Figure it out

& Fix it

Your surprising solution to addiction and substance abuse

By
Mark Turansky

Testimonials*

- *"I wish I could tell the world about this program."*

- *"The curriculum is fresh, exciting and empowering"*

- *"Thank you Mark. You have saved lives."*

- *"I went to church to find recovery and didn't find it, I never thought I would go to recovery and end up finding church."*

- *"I have not felt this healthy and happy in years."*

- *If you seriously want to change or get better and you are ready to work to get better, this program is the program for you."*

- *The New Horizons program is what I would recommend to others. Thank you Mark for everything, everything!!*

- *The New Horizons Choice Process was real and honest and I finally feel free."*

- *"This program is very practical – it's about the nuts and bolts of dealing with addiction.*

- *"As a person who has been in and out of treatment, I can say that this approach will be the "cure" for addiction that everyone has been waiting for."*

- *"I recommend this program because it is a totally different approach and I should know since I have been in and out of treatment programs for the past 8 years."*

*Names have not been included to protect the client's privacy

Foreword

Mark Turansky has a refreshing approach which engages the reader and is very user friendly. His book takes what research has found, translates it into lay language and has created an intervention which is easily understood and simple to implement. It takes the mystery out of addiction and puts the reader in the driver's seat. Finally, a book that respects those with addictions as human beings, capable of making decisions and understanding recovery as being up to the individual – with the tools Mark has provided. I can see this approach being useful for many of life's dilemmas. The simple sentence and life approach he gives provides a way of getting through the tough times in life while growing in one's spirituality and understanding and achieving "wholeness" and that sense of one's true, and beautiful self.

Mark has masterfully laid out the steps that many, over the years, have "confounded" with psychological and research terms that very few would relate to nor understand. Mark's book even provides the path to go deeper with a mentor or professional to support along the way.

It's a must read book that chips away at the stigma society has created around these wonderful, talented, bright and loving people.

Lisa Cook, LSW, ACSW, CSAPA
Executive Director. Kū Aloha Ola Mau Treatment Center Oahu
December 30th, 2013

Copyright information

Figure it, Face it and Fix it: Your surprising solution to addictions and substance abuse
Copyright ©2013
Mark Turansky

Cover photography – Photo of the author at Alii Beach park, Haleiwa, Hawaii. Special thanks to photographer Jon Moore from Hawaii Family Photo (www.hawaiifamilyphoto.com)

Cover Design – Val Horne Graphic Designer from VFX horneshome@hawaii.rr.com

Table of Contents

Dedication

I dedicate this book to my wife Cheryl, who with her quiet strength, has shown me how to live – how to REALLY live.

"...and I will ask Mark to run away with me and we will go from interesting place to interesting place until we find the perfect place to be ourselves."

(Cheryl Turansky)

Acknowledgements

I would like to thank those who helped make this book a reality: Katy Kok and Lori Gossard for the program outline as well as their wisdom and guidance. My wife Cheryl, thank you for sticking with me all these years. My son Jason, whom I taught "how to drink," but who had the inner strength to not follow my negative example. My daughter Taylor whose insight and wisdom never cease to amaze me. My daughter Rylie whose positive spirit of encouragement flows into my soul and creates the lifeblood I need to continue pressing forward.

A special thank you to those, who by their editing skills, toiled alongside of me trying to make head or tail of what I attempt to write: Colin Clyne, Chris "The Comma King" Armstrong, Patricia Ellis and my wife Cheryl who knows how to turn a phrase just as well as she turned my head back in 1979. Thank you for taking what I wrote, "wordsmithing" it, and coming out with a much better presentation. You are awesome!

Preface

"Would you smoke pot with me?" I was 13 years old living in southern California and it was my first day of 8th grade. For some it's the constant peer pressure that works you over and then you succumb. Not for me; I sought it out. I picked one of the school "bad boys" and asked the question that would begin my journey of drug and alcohol abuse for the next 20 years. Recreational pot smoking and occasional beer drinking gave way to an endless array of uppers, downers, cocaine and LSD.

As I matured, I seemed to grow out of the illegal drug use, as one might grow out of teenage fads or a prom outfit. I ended up, however, exchanging one type of addiction for another, as a "beer or two" on the weekends led to a six pack every night. As my drinking buddies and I used to say, "Wine is fine - beer will bring you cheer - but liquor is quicker." Shots of tequila became my drink of choice. They quickly and efficiently brought on the familiar 'buzz' of self-medicating liquid comfort.

It's not that I didn't seek help along the way. I took an alcohol education class, signed up for an online "freedom" course, and went to private counseling. I memorized Bible verses, submitted to "accountability" partners, and fell on my face before God in prayer.

Initially, I had the most success by attending a local Alcoholic Anonymous program. I really loved being with a group of people and getting the support I needed. I participated in that 12-step program for probably a year, and then I was clean and sober for quite some time. But after a few years I thought, *"You know, I've got a handle on this, I learned my lesson."* I remember one Christmas Eve I started drinking again thinking, *"This is the time! It's Christmas Eve. It's okay to have a drink on Christmas Eve! I have learned my lesson, I can be moderate."* Now "off the wagon," I returned to drinking again, but this time I went underground.

I was a closet drinker. The social and religious circles in which I ran would have easily tolerated "moderation," but my appetite for drinking had long since passed that ambiguous line of demarcation. I was leading a double life: the ideal father, husband and people-helper on the outside, but on the inside I was dying a slow death. Spending hundreds of dollars on booze, weaving webs of deceit, and carefully scheduling each drink slowly took its toll on every ounce of self- esteem and pride that I had. I finally hit bottom.

As the ancient proverb says, *"When the student is ready the teacher will appear."* It took a lot to make that phone call but I knew I needed help. On the other line was

Katy Kok (pronounced "cook") from New Horizons Counseling. I will never forget her first words to me: *"We are here to help you, not to judge you."*

I know now that our phone conversation was a divine appointment from the sovereign God of the universe. Her gentle and wise approach resonated with my soul. At first I was her client, then her friend, and finally a colleague. I want to thank Katy and her sister Lori for entrusting their practice to me and allowing me to interpret it in my own way. Many of the thoughts and ideas presented in this book were inspired by these amazing women. The world is a better place because of their contribution. I am grateful to God for their presence in my life.

Over the years I have added many dimensions to the program that I now call "The Choice Process," but the foundation and basic premise that were scribbled on a yellow pad from two sisters sitting on a California beach in the 70's remain the same.

Mark Turansky
Executive Director
New Horizons Counseling
2012

Introduction

Let's talk about what this book is NOT about. The material in this book is not based on the traditional 12-step program. This is not because the 12-step program isn't useful to many; it is. 12-step programs have been around for a long time as a genuine lifeline and a place to turn for those self-destructing from addiction, and I myself have benefitted from it. However, I have discovered that there is a world of difference between MANAGING an addiction and being FREE from addiction. I wanted to be free, unafraid, whole, and healed. This is what I found in the New Horizons "Choice Process" paradigm: the ticket to a "life-do-over." If you want more than a life of managing and struggling with an addiction, then come with me on this journey. It's hard work for sure, but together we will find the light at the end of the tunnel – because there is one.

Other than private counseling, 12-step programs have been the "staple" for treatment worldwide for a long while. Understandably, the 12-step philosophy has become common knowledge to most. Ideas like: "If you are an alcoholic you would never go into a bar." Or, "Those with addictions have a disease and therefore will always be sick or incurable." These ideas have been around long enough that we don't question whether they are actually valid for today, or if indeed there may be another way to look at the quest to be free from addictions. The Choice Process comes from a very different angle. We don't believe addiction is a life sentence or that addiction must be paid for by a life of avoidance, management or dependence on others for our actions. As you embrace this journey to wellness, you will need to be open to new ways of thinking, feeling, and living. For many, the Choice Process can be quite surprising. For me, it was truly refreshing and a whole new way to view myself, and my addiction, and allowed me hope for the future. If that appeals to you, then get ready to think "outside of the box."

It's been said, *"All truth is God's truth."* Perhaps you picked up this book because you desperately want to know the answer to the questions: "How can I be free from addiction? How can I learn a program that would actually work?" I expect that you will be deeply impacted by the truths discovered through this book and through the New Horizons "Choice Process."

There is a cure for addiction. Like the title of this book suggests, before addiction can be "fixed," you must first "figure" the program, "face" the underlying causes, and address fears of relapse.

Each chapter has a "figure it" or "face it" assignment page. To maximize your learning curve, I encourage you to answer each question and fulfill each assignment. Because of the limited space provided in this book, feel free to use a notepad, journal or computer to record your answers. I invite you to join me on a journey that will lead you to be free from addiction forever. *"I am here to help you, not to judge you."*

Figure it Face it & Fix it

Chapter 1
Forget the Labels

Many of us who have struggled with addiction have a particularly difficult time when we come to the decision of having to determine whether or not to accept the truth about a situation. In many addiction recovery circles, this defining moment is solidified by the adoption of a label: *"I am an alcoholic."* or *"I am a cocaine addict."* Facing and accepting your addiction need not be surrendering to a life of carrying a label that diminishes you or causes you shame or discomfort. Forget the labels. Addiction is simply: "The repeated use of a substance or behavior despite the consequences." Do you or a loved one have a habit that causes discomfort or pain? If you say *"yes,"* then you have an addiction. Don't get caught in the trap of wrestling with the idea that you only need help if you fit stereotypical labels. Many an addict has postponed the journey to wellness because they didn't want to be labeled, or they resisted the idea that they fit the description of a typical alcoholic or drug user. Anyone who has been caught in the slavery of addiction knows this to be true. I have clients that come to me and say: *"I just can't figure this out, I have a wonderful career, I have a wonderful family, I am doing great in all these areas in my life but there is one area in my life I cannot seem to get a handle on, or control--why do I keep doing this behavior over and over again? It makes no sense to me!"* If you have ever struggled with these types of questions, you know the madness addiction can bring.

Perhaps you are on the outside watching the life of a loved one and you see their pathway spiraling down towards utter destruction. You see them losing money, social status, jobs, and relationships. In witnessing all the pain, logically you think: *"Can't you see what you are doing to yourself? You are killing yourself and the people around you are suffering!"* Why do they continue to repeat this destructive behavior over and over? This is addiction. This is the crazy rollercoaster of a life out of control.

By virtue of the fact that you have picked up this book, you are acknowledging the discomfort inside yourself that tells you there is a problem that needs fixing. Some problems can't be fixed alone and addiction is one of them. If you were able to get your addiction under control, you would have done it by now - right? If you have a legal problem, what do you do? You go to a lawyer. If you have a physical problem, what do you do? You see a doctor. So, it only makes sense that if you have a problem with chemical dependency, you would seek help from someone who can help you. So, now is the time to seek assistance and get on the journey to wellness. There can be great discomfort in seeking help. At the outset, it doesn't always feel good, but it is a necessary hill to climb in your recovery. Compared to a lifetime of pain, reaching out is only temporary discomfort. You will soon find relief in collaborating with compassionate others on your journey to wellness.

Compassion, along with an effective program, is what this book is all about. I will show you how to go about adopting a mind-set that will shift your perspective about your addiction, and will help you stop your habitual behaviors in a very positive way.

Watch out for that voice in your head that may try to tell you that you can handle this all by yourself. That's the part of your thinking that prevents you from stopping over and over again. This is not something you need to handle next week or even next month. This is something you need to address right now. I am asking you to make a commitment to deal with your problem, or chances are, you will continue to use and postpone the life and happiness you seek. Ask yourself, *"If I don't do something now, then when will I?"* If you deal with this now, in a positive and effective way, then you can begin to fashion a whole new life for yourself.

Some may define addiction as a bad habit, a psychological compulsion, an obsession, dependence, or disease. But the Bible has a different word for it. If you look in the Bible, you never see the word "addiction," that's the word we use in our culture today. The word the Bible uses to imply addiction is "slavery"-- *"For a man is a slave to whatever has mastered him."*[1] The "master" is the substance and the "slave" is the addict. Anyone who has been caught in the slavery of addiction understands this concept. Those of us who have struggled with addiction know the inner pang of truth that says, *"I am a slave."* There are many kinds of slaves: Slaves to alcohol, slaves to pornography, slaves to anger, slaves to sexual addiction, slaves to food, and countless others. The New Horizons Choice Process is applicable and effective for any form of slavery.

From time to time, I get calls from people who want an assessment to see whether or not they are an alcoholic. Some types of formal substance abuse assessments can be very costly and take several hours. I tell them that we can do the assessment right now, right

---

[1] 2 Peter :19b The New International Version of the Holy Bible

here, on the phone, free of charge! This makes them happy, and so we begin:

Me: *"Okay, are you ready?"*

Caller: *"Yes."*

Me: *"Here is the first question: Do you drink?"*

Caller: *"Yes."*

Me: *"Does your drinking cause you problems?"*

Caller: *"Yes."*

Me: *"Okay, our assessment is over. You are a problem drinker. Let's get started."*

There is often a chuckle on the other end of the line because they get my point. I tell them that I don't care about labels. It doesn't matter to me if you are labeled an alcoholic, a druggie, a pothead, or anything else. What matters, is if the behavior or substance is causing you problems or pain. If it is, then you are not getting what you really want and need: peace of mind, happiness, joy, meaningful relationships, and good health. If your addiction is keeping you from any or all of these qualities, then it's time to get some help!

Figure it out

Definition of Addiction – "The repeated use of a substance

or behavior _____ the consequences."

What enslaves you? (name your addiction)

Chapter 2
This Is My Program

In order for change to happen, a person must be motivated. He or she has to face reality and admit they have a problem. In my practice, I regularly get calls from well-meaning family members and friends who are calling on behalf of a loved one who is struggling with addiction. Often times their first question is: *"How can I help my friend, spouse, son or daughter? They are addicted."* My question to them is: *"Why aren't they calling me? Why are you calling me?"* Then I ask: *"Does your loved one think they need help?"* They will often say: *"Oh no, they don't think they have a problem."* It is at that point that I must break the news to them with as much compassion as I can. *"I appreciate you calling, but the truth is that you have no control over your loved one; and while that can be very frustrating, the person needs to call me and reach out for help themselves."* I always commend a caller for picking up the phone or going online to educate themselves about programs and treatment so they can present to their loved one information when the time is right. It's a sign that they care, and it's something that they CAN do until the person is finally ready to seek help for themselves. Once your loved one is open, then you can share the information and guidance you have found on their behalf. If an individual doesn't think there is a problem, then why would they be motivated to go into a program that's going to "solve their problem" if they don't even think that there is a "problem" in the first place? Sometimes, a painful event occurs and packs the power needed to cause an addict to finally "hit bottom" and they say, *"Okay, I am ready for help!"* However, the bottom line is that you cannot force anybody into treatment with high expectations. In order for TRUE change to happen, a person must be personally motivated. From time to time someone will attend treatment, and during recovery they have an epiphany. In my experience, however, that is the exception rather than the rule.

An award-winning program on TV that has been very successful in recent years is called "Intervention."[2] On the show, addicts are persuaded to be filmed "documentary style," by telling them they're making a film about addiction. But really, the documentary is a set-up to allow concerned friends and family to confront the addicts about their substance abuse. Without the addict's knowledge, the family members gather together in a motel room, and the addicted person is told that they are to come to the motel room to tape their final interview.

---

[2] A&E Network Emmy Award winning program began airing in 2005

When they walk through the door, they are confronted with their family members sitting and staring at them, ready for an intervention. Often times, the person becomes very hostile; they get angry and run into the bathroom or even down the street. Why does this happen? I believe this happens because people feel pinned against the wall. When a person is forced to do something against their will, often times the result will be behavior that may resemble a caged wild animal. Now, sometimes these individuals relent and say they will go to treatment and do go. However, more often than not, you find out at the very end of the show that they never finished treatment or they were kicked out of the program.

You cannot force treatment on someone. People have to go through the pain of addiction, they have to experience the consequences, and they have to hit bottom. Only the pain can bring them to their knees, and when you are on your knees the only place to look is up. That is why we call it *"hitting bottom."* When a client comes to me and says they're at the end of their rope, I tell them that, on the one hand, I am sad for their pain because it's no fun to suffer the consequences of addiction; however, on the other hand, I am grateful for their pain, because it is a good motivator. Pain motivates. It gets us moving. I am not opposed to the "disease model" concerning addiction.

If one likens addiction to heart disease or type 2 diabetes then we see many similarities; all these diseases are lifestyle related. However, even with diabetes and heart disease, many people do not seek help or start changing their lifestyle choices until they experience the physical pain that the disease brings. God has provided the gift of pain so that we do not stay stuck in destructive habits that hurt ourselves and others.

You may be in pain, but struggle with the idea of having to seek help. Consider the following: If you have a problem with your car and you are not a mechanic, you go to a mechanic to get your car fixed. If you want to have your house sold and you don't know anything about real estate, you will go to a realtor to help you sell your home. If you have some kind of legal question, you will go to a lawyer and get advice about the judicial system. We ask for help in all other areas of our life, but a personal problem like addiction seems to be harder for people to extend themselves and receive the help they need. I want you to know that I understand how hard it is to reach out. However, you will never regret seeking assistance. You are worth it. Your life is worth it. The truth is there are some things we just can't do very effectively on our own. Breaking free from addiction often requires someone who "has been there" to come alongside and guide you to success. There is no one like a person who has been freed from their addiction, who can identify with and understand your struggle. Together with the Choice Process, you and a trusted advisor, counselor or friend can negotiate your journey to freedom with compassion and a solid proven program for success.

When a client sits in my office for the first session, I spend a considerable amount of time talking to them about their motivation for conquering their addiction. They are, in essence, going through a time of purification, which involves a process which I call "scrubbing", in other words cleaning up their motivation for doing the work they need to do. It's essential that they do this for themselves, and not because someone else expects them to. Over the years, I have realized that proper motivation is a secret to the longevity of commitment to sobriety. If one is to achieve success in the long term, it is foundational that they enter into their journey for themselves. If someone comes to my office and they want to go through the program but they are saying things like: *"My wife gave me an ultimatum-- she says that if I don't go to treatment then we are going to break up"* or, *"I tested hot on a random urine analysis test at work and my boss says they will fire me if I don't enroll in treatment,"* then we need to take a closer look at what is truly motivating this person. An important statement I make clear for a client is, *"This is your program."* You have to do this for yourself; you have to take personal ownership and declare, *"This is my program."*

I don't know if you have ever tried stopping an addiction to please someone else, but if you have, you'll probably agree that this type of motivation can be shaky. When you try to stop an addiction for someone else, it is their opinion of you that matters most, and others' opinions of you can change from day to day. This can lead to resentment and discouragement if you are not being appreciated or affirmed for your efforts at sobriety. Doing a program for someone else is not the kind of motivation that will bring you success in the long run.

While it's true that if an individual gets clean and sober others around them will also benefit, that alone cannot be the primary motivating factor. This is not your wife's program. This is not your boss's program. This is not the court's program. If you are my client, I don't want you invested in impressing me, your counselor – Why? This is not my program, this is YOUR program. You need the inner conviction of wanting to make the change for yourself. The one true reason to enter into a program for addiction that will speak to your heart and soul is, *"I want to be free from addiction for me because I am worth it."*

When you can say that, you will be ready to change for YOU, regardless of whom or what circumstances change around you. That is a solid foundation to changing your life for good.

I want you to know that this is one time in your life when it is okay to be focused on yourself. I know that many of us have been taught that it's never okay to be selfish, but this is not selfishness. This is self-love and self-care, which are two very healthy and admirable qualities. The truth about proper motivation is this: If there is any time in life that is okay to be selfish, it's when an individual goes through the treatment and recovery journey. This is your program; you need to do it for you!

The statement and conviction that *this is my program* is the foundation and stabilizer of your journey. We need to support you in that by helping you to keep it to yourself. For a time, keeping it to yourself is a way to keep motivation pure and to keep you on the right track. What I mean by keeping it to yourself is to do your work with an internal focus. If you are following the principles in this book, the Choice Process approach will slowly unfold before you and make complete sense. However, other people in your life who are not reading this book or going through the program may lack clarity and understanding about your process. This can be a distraction from your inner work. Sometimes when someone starts a treatment program, they might want to impress the loved ones in their life by going home and talking about it. But again, we need to keep our motivations pure and focus on ourselves and the work at hand, not pleasing others. There will be plenty of time to share your journey with those you love once you have completed your program and are in a better place. Until then, simply let them know you are focusing on your process. Tell them that you appreciate their support, and that you will share with them your journey when the time is right. Then you can be free to shout it from the rooftops!

Remember these two statements: *"This is my program." "Keep it to yourself."*

Figure it out

A person must be _____ for change to happen.

> ➤ I must _____ that I need help – If I don't think I have an addiction problem then what is there to work on?

> ➤ Keep it to _____. This needs to be "your program." Stopping for someone else will not work.

> ➤ It's okay to be _____ .

In order to help you to define and identify your personal motivation complete the following exercise:

DIRECTIONS: Imagine your life completely devoid of your problem or addiction. What would be the benefits you would enjoy from NOT using? Take some time and really think this through. Make a COMPLETE list. Start by using the area below, but use a separate piece of paper if you need to.

1. _____

2. _____

3. _____

4. _____

5. _____

6. _____

7. _____

8. _____

Chapter 3
C.B.T.
God's natural design for change

Cognitive Behavior Therapy (CBT) is a systematic approach to changing the way we think, that ultimately affects our actions. CBT is the understanding that our thoughts and beliefs will ultimately determine our behavior. As the mind processes information experientially, convictions develop. These convictions determine how you and I act. So, my behavior is not determined by external things like people, situations, and events; but by an internal conviction system that has been developed over time.

Now, why is this important? This is important because we CAN change the way we can feel and act, despite our surroundings. This is a VERY profound truth; read it again.

All addictions have one thing in common. It doesn't matter if it's shopping, alcohol, pornography, gambling or drugs. When a person "uses" there is a release of "feel good" chemicals in the brain called endorphins and dopamine. These brain chemicals create the good feelings, and if I can find a predictable way to feel good, I may become psychologically dependent on whatever is creating that wonderful feeling. God created these chemical reactions within us so that you and I can enjoy a day at the amusement park, a kiss from a lover, an embrace from your child, or any of the many pleasurable activities that *naturally* release these "feel-good" chemicals in our brain.

Here is the good news: The very chemicals that move along our synapses to create these addictive habits, can also be harnessed to change our behavior from destructive patterns to a more constructive lifestyle. God has designed our brain for change. We can "re-wire" the way we think. This can be done through a systematic process that counselors and psychologists call "Cognitive Behavioral Therapy."

So how does CBT work in the brain? In order to describe different personality types we often use this terminology: *"He is a right-brain person or she is a left-brain person"* When we think of a "right-brain" person, we think of someone who is artistic, who seems to have the ability to think more abstractly and creatively than others. We might describe a "left-brain" person as more analytical. We use these terms in our culture to describe how we tend to approach life. The truth of the matter is that people don't just exclusively use only their left or right brain hemisphere. The brain is a complete unit and works interactively throughout the various lobes and hemispheres as it has been designed. The brain is very complex and although I am not a neurologist, in order to explain how CBT works, I am going to use the right-brain and left-brain analogy to help us understand the complexity of the process of behavioral change.

Let's think of the left-brain as the processor of information. Perhaps we can call it "the information center." Using this analogy, we can visualize the left brain like it's a big computer or file cabinet system that stores all the facts and figures of life. All the information you need to make a decision is stored in these files. Let's say that we had a file in there that says: "Airplanes." All the information that you've ever learned about airplanes is in that filing cabinet or that file folder in the left side of your brain: What kind of planes there are, everything you know about airlines, and everything you know about buying a ticket and booking a flight. So, the left-hand side of the brain is stocked full with information and data concerning airplanes.

In contrast, the "right-hand" side of the brain is where you have processed your experiences related to airline flight. For instance, as soon as you read the word "airplane," all the information and experiences you have had with flight are brought to the surface of your brain, into your consciousness. Perhaps you have been flying all your life and your experience with planes has been mostly positive: They transport you to see loved ones, they help you with your business, and you enjoy first class. The thought of going on a flight is positive and you look forward to your next trip. On the other hand, you may be someone who has a fear of flying; just the thought of getting on an airplane makes you feel queasy and sick to your stomach. Perhaps you took a flight when you were younger and there was extreme turbulence on that flight. Some people who were not buckled into their seat belts hit their heads on the ceiling and had to be transported off the plane via a stretcher when the flight landed; so your experience with airplanes has been traumatic.

So, let's say that you had this terrifying turbulence experience when you were five years old and you have a great fear of flying. Now I come alongside of you and I give you all sorts of information about airplanes, how I grew up flying all my life because I live in Hawaii, and how air travel is really the safest mode of travel in the world, statistically speaking. Do you think that information from me is going to change your mind about how scary airplanes are? Not likely, because the experience you personally had is going to override any information I might provide. Don't you think that a person who is afraid of flying looks out in the world and sees people who fly every day? They see that other people enjoy airplanes and flying to distant places, but that makes no difference to them, because of their personal experience with flight. So, we have a right-hand side of the brain that's more experiential, and we have a left-hand side that's more informational; and together, they create this three-dimensional picture of the reality that we have when it comes to airplanes.

The airplane analogy is a helpful, though simplistic example of how our brain works. In addition, we need to understand that the right-hand side of the brain is the executive control center of the brain. It's this "right side" of experience that dictates how we make decisions. Nothing gets to the left-hand side of the brain without passing through the right side first. And this is why CBT is so powerful, because it's not just about information. If making behavioral change was just about gaining more information, then all I would need to do say is *"Stop it! Your addiction is hurting you!"* and you would stop. However, we all know it doesn't work that way. <u>Lasting change happens through an experiential process that enables an individual to create inward convictions that, in turn, result in behavioral change</u>. Read that again.

This explains why there are so many education programs out there that aren't effective because many people think that educational (information) programs are all that are needed to stop addictive behavior. Campaigns like *"Just say no"* and commercials like: *"This is your brain. This is your brain on drugs."* (Remember the video of an egg frying in a pan?) are examples of this. DUI offenders are sentenced to alcohol education classes and are given information about what alcohol does to the brain or what drugs do to your body – all of which are valuable, but ultimately doesn't change behavior.

Cognitive Behavior Therapy has been around for several decades now. Some people thought that it was created in the 60's[3], but I think that the Bible teaches the original form of CBT. The Bible says, *"Do not conform any longer to the pattern of this world but be transformed by the renewing of your mind!"* [4] Why does the apostle Paul call us to this mind transformation process? It is because God has created us with the ability to transform or renew our mind, and we do that through this cognitive method. Over time, healing occurs as we transform our thoughts. The process starts with information, and then travels

---

[3] © Copyright, 2008, by the National Association of Cognitive-Behavioral Therapists.
[4] Romans 12:2a NIV version of The Holy Bible

down to my "gut" for experiential processing, and after that is deposited into my heart as conviction.

Let's look at a simple illustration that may be helpful: Think back to when you were 4 years old. You are in your kitchen with your mother who is cooking dinner on the stove. As you are playing under your mom's feet, you are getting a little bit too close to the stove, and the stove-top is cherry-red. So mom says to you: *"Honey, don't touch the stove! If you touch the stove you will get burned."* Now, that's information isn't it? So you take that information into the left hand side of your brain. Even as a 4-year old you process the information and come to the conclusion: *"You know mom usually tells me things that are true and she is believable,"* and so you store that information. But for a foolish four year old, is that enough? Not usually. Mom then walks out of the kitchen to answer the phone and out of curiosity you touch that hot stove. Immediately, pain happens and you get burned.

Well, guess what? CBT just happened – an immediate thing. What happened in that moment, was the information that mom gave you was then processed experientially through the pain of touching the hot stove, and then deposited into your heart and resulted in a life-long-conviction that says, *"I don't want to touch a hot stove anymore!"* You see? Now I have a conviction, nobody has to tell me anymore not to touch a hot stove. Now, I don't want to touch a hot stove.

CBT is really just the normal way you and I process our choices and beliefs from information to conviction all the time. This natural CBT process can result in what we call "wisdom and maturity."

On the day of my 16th birthday, I got my driver's license. At that time I was mixed up with a bunch of guys who were full of testosterone but very little wisdom or maturity. We wanted to race our cars, but of course it wasn't my car, it was my parents' car! We would go screaming down the road, sliding around corners, and I ended up crashing my parent's car and getting traffic tickets for speeding.   Meanwhile, I was under my father's insurance policy and his rates started to increase due to my negligence. So he had the idea to bring me down to the insurance company headquarters and have his agent talk to me. When I arrived, the helpful gentleman talked to me about the dangers of driving fast. He gave me statistics about my age bracket and demographic and how many fatalities happen when teens drive fast. He suggested tactics like taking back roads, being content to drive slowly, and taking in the scenery as I drove around town.

What I got was information, right? Do you think that changed me? Absolutely not! As soon as I got out of that meeting, I continued to drive as before, and as time went by, I crashed more cars and got more speeding tickets. This went on for several years, and during that time I was paying out lots of dollars. Every time I crashed the car, my parents made me pay for it and I experienced the pain of the pocket book. I also experienced the pain of having to pay extra insurance and the fines from traffic tickets. Over time, finally I decided that it might be a better idea if I just slowed down a little bit. I bought myself an old 1941 Willy's Jeep, and I remember driving down the road and thinking: *"I like this... I got this vehicle that really can't go fast and it forces me to go slow."* It finally dawned on me, while traveling in the right lane of the freeway at 54 miles an hour, that I hadn't gotten a ticket for a long time.

This is an example of Cognitive Behavior Therapy. When I experientially went through the pain and consequences of my actions, my brain enhanced the information I already knew by impressing on me the "down-sides" to speeding. Also, and perhaps most important, was the experience of the "up-sides" to not speeding which solidified my ability to change my behavior. Now, I don't recklessly speed any longer. The "old Mark" liked to drive fast, but the "new Mark" has changed. That's what CBT does: As a result of going through the process of taking in information and experiencing the consequences and benefits of my behavior, I could embrace what I call "the new me," or, the "new Mark." I look at those old behaviors and I say: *"They have passed away. This is not something I want to do; it's not part of my desired reality. I now embrace "the new me."* Now I enjoy driving around with no fear: No fear of being pulled over by the policeman, no fear of crashing my car because of negligent driving, no fear of hurting myself or others because of my poor choices, and no fear of my insurance rates increasing. Now that I have totally embraced these convictions in my life, I don't want to go back to being a reckless and out of control driver. That's Cognitive Behavior Therapy at work. It's maturity. It's wisdom. It's a natural way to make changes. It's God's design.

You have probably heard, as I have, of stories about people who have struggled for years with some kind of addiction and then testify that *"One day I woke up and all the desire was gone, and I haven't used since."* Can this happen? Well, yes and no. More than likely they went through their own personal course of CBT and didn't even know it. When someone is a slave to an addiction and they wake up each morning kicking themselves and self-loathing their addictive ways for many years, sometimes those powerful negative emotions can culminate into a distinct moment of being able to override the desire to continue using. While it may seem like it was just out of the blue, if they really took time to inventory the process, they might find that there was much more behind their decision to quit than they realize. While it would be wonderful to wake up one morning without a desire to use one's substance of choice, realistically most of us need to be intentional about changing our lives. Fortunately, with the Choice Process, we can do just that and it need not take years to accomplish.

If I have an addiction, I am destroying and wasting my life. I need to start getting clean and sober right away. The Choice Process uses a structured CBT format to speed up the process so it doesn't take months or years to get where you want to be. The Choice Process is a systematic program that uses the natural way God has wired our brain to our best advantage. This book and this approach is designed to quickly and efficiently help you to be able to change the way you think, which will result in changed behavior. Once you begin to enjoy the benefits of not being enslaved by your destructive habits, you can then embrace "the new me" and live a life free from addiction.

Figure it out

- C.B.T. is a _____ approach
  to changing the way we _____ which
  will ultimately affect our _____.

Behavior change will not happen through
_____ alone.

The brain takes in information, processes it experientially
and deposits it into the heart as _____.

Chapter 4
The Choice Process - an overview

So let's get started, shall we? The CBT process for change that we will utilize is called, The Choice Process. The Choice Process has six phrases that represent the backbone of the program. These phrases are the core of your treatment. From here forward, as I refer to the Choice Process, I want you to remember that I am talking about these six phrases. When I work with clients I give them a small poker chip style of token with the six phrases printed on it. The token is designed to be carried in your pocket, so you can memorize the phrases and say them over and over, word for word. The Choice Process phraseology is designed to remind you of all the teachings and truth you will discover in this program. As we go through each phrase, you will be given assignments that will take the program information and help you to experience feelings about what you value. This will ultimately lead to new convictions and behavior that will help you to get what you want out of life, instead of what you do not want. (This is the essence of CBT)

Of the six phrases, the first three are "truth statements" and the last three are "declarative statements." In other words, the first three phrases remind you of the truth and reality of your situation. The final three statements declare the action points that will lead you to freedom from your addiction.

The Choice Process addresses all of the various types of addictions: Alcohol, drug, shopping, gambling, video gaming, and even internet pornography. The word "use" in the first two phrases (I want to use. I can use.) is a catch-all phrase for whatever your particular addiction may be. I encourage you to throw out the word "use" and insert a word that represents your habit. So, if your addiction is alcohol you could say, *"I want to drink. I can drink."* If your addiction is smoking crack cocaine then you could say, *"I want to smoke. I can smoke."* If your addiction is smoking pot then you might say, *"I want to burn. I can burn."* If your addiction is shopping you could say, *"I want to shop. I can shop."* You get the idea. I want you to custom design it to your own struggle.

For the sake of simplicity, I am going to design most of my illustrations and use of the application of the Choice Process around alcohol abuse. Although the Choice Process works with all types of addiction, problem drinking is by far the most common habit that walks into my office.

Each of these six phrases is designed to accomplish a goal. Also, each of the six phrases will remind you of one or more truths that will be taught in this book. These are the six phrases and their corresponding goals:

> ➤ **"I want to use"**- This truth phrase helps to break you out of the tendency to repress the urge to use, and acknowledges the truth of your situation.

> ➤ **"I can use"** - This truth phrase helps you break the cycle of deprivation in which stopping is punishment and using again becomes a reward.

> ➤ **"However, once and it's over"** – What's over? Your benefits of sobriety. This truth phrase helps you to become aware of false confidence and reminds you of the reality that all the work you have done can be erased through relapse.

> ➤ **"So in this moment"** - This declaration phrase helps you become aware of your own tendency towards self-sabotage and reminds you of your "Junkie Mind."

> ➤ **"I choose to accept temporary discomfort"** - This declaration phrase helps the stopping process become positive instead of negative and helps instill the life skill of delayed gratification.

> ➤ **"To get my benefits."** - This declaration phrase is the "engine of motivation," the catalyst that will bring success in your journey.

The next six chapters will deal with each of these phrases in detail. Within each chapter you will be given an assignment to complete. In order for the CBT process to work, you must complete each one of the homework assignments. Take the time to think things through. Each assignment is designed for you to "experience" the information that is being presented. Remember, the key to change is not just more information. It is experiencing that information so that you will develop conviction. So please, don't skip over these sections without doing the work; they are crucial steps to your freedom.

The Choice Process phraseology is designed to help you "brainwash" yourself. In other words "wash" out the old, unhealthy thinking patterns and replace them with healthy ones. I'm not brainwashing you, the book isn't brainwashing you, the program isn't brainwashing you; you need to brainwash yourself. So, I want you to memorize the phrases of the Choice Process word for word. When I meet with a client, I always start each session with them saying the six statements to me. I'll know they have really internalized the material when the phrases roll off their tongue perfectly. I am a stickler for word for word perfection. Each word is "pregnant" with meaning, and we don't want to change, alter or modify anything, with the exception of the word "use." I encourage you to type out the Choice Process on a piece of paper and put it in your pocket or purse, and take it out over and over during the day to learn and memorize it. (or, if you have received a token from your New Horizons counselor make sure to carry it with you wherever you go.) I sometimes give my clients small colored adhesive dots you can buy at any office supply store to put up around their home, work and vehicle. No one else knows what the dots are for, but they will serve as a reminder for you to say the Choice Process throughout the day. Especially for the first couple of weeks, I want you to say the Choice Process at least 100 times daily until it simply becomes a part of you. Say it when you wake-up, eat breakfast, between breakfast and lunch, at lunch, between lunch and dinner, at dinner and after dinner and the last thing before bed.

Right now, these phrases probably do not hold much meaning. However, by the time you have successfully completed the program, they will have become very profound to you. As you go through the material you will quickly begin to recognize that the

Choice Process is really a life skill. The principles on this token and in this book will have far reaching implications in your life. Not just for your addiction, but also in any area you desire a sense of control and consistency. You can use these principles for quitting smoking, dieting, reaching a goal that has been elusive, or even anger management. In the next chapter we will explore the meaning behind the first of the six Choice Process phrases.

Figure it out

There are six phrases in the Choice Process. The first three are _____ statements and the final three are _____statements.

To customize the Choice Process to my own challenge, I will substitute the word "use" for_____

In order for you to change your thinking you must _____ these phrases word for word.

It's time to grab your token and recite your Choice Process. Read it out loud several times: *"I want to use, I can use, however once and it's over. So in this moment I choose to accept temporary discomfort so I can get my benefits."*

Chapter 5

"I want to use"

Taking personal responsibility

Picture each phrase of the Choice Process like dominoes. When the first one falls, it hits the next and then that one hits the subsequent domino until they all fall down. That is how these phrases work. It starts with the first truth phrase, and then builds and builds until the thought is complete.

"I want to use." Why is this statement important? Answer: It acknowledges the truth about your situation. Truth is reality, if you don't live in reality you do not live in truth. Often times when people struggle with addiction to alcohol or drugs they will come to a place where they "hit bottom." Usually this is a final painful event that has knocked them to their knees: A spouse threatens to leave or files for divorce. The person is arrested for something related to their addiction (DUI, theft, domestic violence, CPS gets involved, etc.) or there is a significant loss of money or a health scare. So by the time they seek out help, they are a wreck. The tears flow, remorse and regret are overwhelming, and the reality of losing everything they have worked so hard for and everything they care about, is hanging by a frayed and worn thread.

It is not uncommon for an individual in these circumstances to say, *"I never want to use again."* In that moment, the pain is so great that the thought of using and returning to their addiction seems far away and the idea of returning to the addictive behavior is preposterous. They can't imagine that they would EVER use again, and so they may proclaim, *"I'm done!"*

But as one of my clients used to say, *"I have a built-in-forgetter."* In the painful moments, we tend to swear off our addictions. However, as soon as the threat of consequence is lifted and the sting of the pain starts to fade into a distant memory, the "built-in-forgetter" will kick in, and we will return to our old ways.

Often times when the pain is acute and a person cannot imagine themselves returning to their addiction, they have a hard time accepting this first phrase "I want to use." *"But I don't want to use anymore,"* they will protest. The fact of the matter is, what they really don't want any more of, is the consequences of their addiction. Separating the substance or behavior from the consequences is a very important aspect of understanding why we say, *"I want to use."*

To help you to make this distinction, I'm going to use the following illustration: Let's say you and I make "The Perfect Alcoholic Drink." We call it "Perfection." Why is it perfect? It's free, it causes no health problems, the high is wonderful but you are not impaired in any way that would cause you embarrassment; in fact, you are more alert and productive. If you are pulled over by an officer, the substance would not show up on a standard blood alcohol content (B.A.C.) test that might otherwise get you arrested. Now, wouldn't you want to own stock in "Perfection?" We would make billions, just open the cash drawer and rake it all in. Most people would answer, *"Yes"* and that helps us to understand the difference between not wanting to drink, and not wanting the consequences that come from drinking.

When we say, *"I don't want to ever use again."* It's true to a certain extent, because anyone who has experienced the ugly side of addiction will say: "I don't want to do this anymore; I don't want to ever experience pain and fear like this again." In actuality, what really is going on inside of them is a war. Part of us doesn't want to do it anymore, but there is a part that lies dormant at the moment, and if we do not acknowledge that part of us that DOES want to use we are setting ourselves up for possible future relapse.

37

In the Bible, the apostle Paul talks about this inward war that he himself fought: *"It seems to be a fact of life that when I want to do what is right, I inevitably do what is wrong. I love to do God's will so far as my new nature is concerned. But there is something else deep within me, in my lower nature that is at war with my mind and wins the fight and makes me a slave to the sin that is still within me."*[5] Paul is describing our inner war. I want to, but part of me doesn't want to. Paul admits it, and we need to admit it as well; because it's reality. We must not live in denial about our addiction.

Becoming addicted to something does not happen overnight. By the time someone steps into my office for treatment they have spent months, sometimes many years nursing their habit. Months and years of behavior drill down deep into our soul and psyche and become a part of who we are. These tendencies just don't dry up and go away overnight. When a person has been using for months and years they are like an ocean liner steaming ahead toward destruction. Turning a large ship is no easy task. We expect it will take time for a ship to alter its course, but given the time, it will surely do so. This is true for you and I as well. So, when we say, *"I want to use,"* we accept

---

the fact that it is normal for us to want to use; there is no need to feel guilty. Merely wanting to use doesn't mean that I'm going to; it just acknowledges the reality of my situation.

So, the first phrase of the Choice Process helps us take personal responsibility. If I say, *"I don't want to use,"* then there is no problem. And if there is no problem there is no need for a book like this, or for treatment, counseling, a program or rehab. When we do not acknowledge reality and truth we call that "living in denial." I deal with people who have been in an addictive behavior sometimes months and others for years, perhaps 20 years or more in some cases. Regardless of how long you have been using, the first step to loosening the knot of which you are bound, is to make peace with the desire to use. We are living in denial when we don't accept that, and it is the truth which sets you free. Because of this, saying *"I want to use"* helps us to move towards freedom.

Assignment: Let's pause for a moment and complete a very important assignment. Take a moment and think of all the "good" parts of your addiction. What is your "payoff?" How does it make you feel? Do you seem to be able to do certain things better when you are using? What enjoyment does it bring? Be honest. There probably are several things you can list here. One does not return again and again to their addiction unless there is some kind of reward. Make your list below:

_____

_____

_____

_____

_____

_____

_____

_____

_____

Now, take a moment and look at your list. These are the reasons "I want to use" is true for you. A lot of times, people who are stuck in the slavery of addiction continue the cycle by trying to stop and then starting again. They can repeat this pattern for years. Then they finally ask themselves: *"Why do I keep doing this?"* The consequences, once again, start mounting in their lives and then, again, they ask themselves: *"I don't know why I keep doing this; there is so much pain in my life, why do I keep doing this over and over again?"* I point to their list and say, *"This is why..."*

Admitting to yourself that you want to use helps you understand why your mind keeps obsessing about the addictive behavior. It helps you understand why you keep worrying and thinking about a future opportunity where you might be in a position to use again. Why do you obsess about these things? *Because you want to use.*

Let's say I've enjoyed a period of abstinence. I've decided to stop, but then I start to worry and obsess to myself: *"What about the future? Pretty soon I will be going away on this business trip, what if I use?"* OR, *"I am supposed to be the best man or maid of honor at my friend's upcoming wedding. Everyone is going to be drinking, what if that triggers me?"* Or, *"My spouse is going to be going out of town soon, and I am going to be home alone-will I use?"* – These are all opportunities for your mind to start obsessing and worrying. Understand this very important concept. The only reason you are obsessing about these future opportunities is because

YOU WANT TO USE! It's okay, you're not bad for wanting to use. You're not hopeless because you want to use. You are just human.

Once you accept the fact that a part of you wants to use, it allows you to rise up and no longer repress the truth. Recall that it is truth that sets us free, so we need to have a foundation built on truth, not repressing or fearing the truth.

What is repression? The American Heritage Dictionary defines repression as: *"The unconscious exclusion of painful impulses, desires, or fears from the conscious mind."* Take a moment now and picture your brain as it sits in your skull, like a large wrinkled walnut. When you are actually thinking about a particular thought, imagine that thought literally sitting on top of your mind. So, if I said, *"think about being teased when you were young,"* the thought of being teased climbed up from your subconscious mind, where it was hidden out of view, to sit on top of your brain where you are now thinking about it. It's not that you haven't ever contemplated when you were teased as a child before; the visual memories of being teased and the thoughts about being teased were buried deep in the subconscious part of your brain. All that was needed to retrieve them was a suggestion.

With that example in mind it's easy to understand repression. When you are thinking a thought, it is there at the top of your brain. But, when you repress a thought, and are not thinking about it consciously, it has not gone away either. It's still down in our subconscious where we cannot face and deal with it. The thought will lie dormant, like a sleeping volcano waiting to erupt.

Before I have you spend some time practicing this truth, let's take a look at one of the more common, down sides to addiction-- financial consequences. Money is a big one, right? The amount of money that an addiction can rob out of your pocket is stunning when you sit down and figure it out. Consider the following exercise I go through in our alcohol education program for someone who has been arrested for a DUI. First we start counting up all the dollars of how much their arrest cost: The fines, getting their car out of impound, paying court fees, lawyer fees, alcohol education course fees. That dollar amount often can be in the thousands. Then they have to take into consideration how much their insurance will be raised each year because this DUI is now on their record. Let's say we come to a total of $7000 dollars. Then I ask them how many drinks they had that night, *"Well, I probably had 10,"* they say. We divide the total cost of their financial output by the number of drinks they had. In this case it cost my client about 700 dollars per drink! They will shake their heads as the financial reality of their using sinks in.

Assignment: Take a moment now and write down all the consequences and pain that the addiction brings into your life. I really want you to take time to think this through – use a separate sheet of paper if necessary. You might want to have main categories and then sub categories under the main heading. The most common consequences will fit under the following categories: financial consequences, relationship consequences, health consequences, self-image consequences, spiritual consequences, legal consequences and career consequences. There are many others, but these are most often the main ones mentioned.

_____

_____

_____

_____

_____

_____

_____

_____

_____

_____

Compare the list you just made (consequences of addiction) with the list you made on the previous page (the benefits of addiction). The comparison is striking isn't it? The laundry list of consequences always outweighs the benefits – most of the time two or three consequences to every single benefit listed.

"I want to use" is a statement of truth. When I admit the truth, I am living in reality. Living in reality allows me to take the personal responsibility that I need to in order to face and fix my problem. That's what this program is all about. When I say, *"I want to use"* I'm bringing truth to the surface, facing the problem, taking personal responsibility, and moving forward towards freedom. You are doing well. You have taken another positive step towards the life you want. I am proud of you.

Figure it out

I _____ to use (this statement helps break the cycle of repression)

Admitting "I want to use" acknowledges the _____ about my situation.

Admitting "I want to use" enables me to take _____ responsibility

Admitting "I want to use" helps me understand the "why" behind my mind's _____ about the future

Admitting "I want to use" brings me to reality, I am no longer living in _____ about my addiction.

Admitting "I want to use" recognizes that I am weak, so I can then get the _____ that I need

It's time to grab your token and recite your Choice Process. Read it out loud several times:

"I want to use, I can use, however once and it's over. So in this moment I choose to accept temporary discomfort so I can get my benefits."

Chapter 6

"I can use..."

Empowering your ability to choose

Every Christmas there is a parade in my community. The parade route happens to circle the particular neighborhood where I live. There are three ways in and out of my neighborhood where my house is located. On one particular December Saturday, I was returning home on my regular route and found the parade had begun. Hoping to avoid it, I swung a U turn and went to plan B –unfortunately it was blocked as well. When I arrived at the last of my three alternatives, and found that road to be blocked as well, I knew I was out of options and conceded to watching the parade from my vehicle, instead of getting home to start my Saturday chores.

Most people who struggle with addiction try a variety of methods or techniques designed to break the slavery the habit has trapped them in. Let's say your struggle is with alcohol. First, you try cutting back. Then you make little rules for yourself: *"I will only drink on the weekends. I will only drink on special occasions. I will limit myself to only two or three drinks when I go out. I will only drink beer – not the hard stuff."* As each rule is made and then compromised you slip deeper and deeper into the addictive pattern that brings misery. This pattern of trying to quit on your own is all too common, and it exposes one main roadblock most people experience when trying to stop an addictive behavior called, "The Cycle of Deprivation."

The Cycle of Deprivation is characterized by certain sentiments or emotions that you experience when you feel you "can't" do something. Feelings like anger, frustration, irritability or that you are missing out on all the fun. Almost everyone who has been caught in the slavery of addiction goes through this cycle. The cycle usually begins with the pain that addiction brings into your life, as it does for everyone sooner or later. If you drink too much you are going to experience a hangover, health issues, and disruption to your life. Your time will be compromised, and your integrity will begin to slip as you find yourself lying and covering your tracks. So, you decide you want to stop. This is good, but the problem now is that the stopping process feels negative. You feel like you are missing out and not having fun. You might find you can "white knuckle" it with willpower for a while, but then finally give in to your cravings. This is The Cycle of Deprivation completed. When you were desperately holding on to your sobriety, you were miserable; when you gave in to your addiction it was pleasurable. In this cycle, the sobriety feels like a <u>punishment</u>, while the using again felt like a <u>reward</u>. This is part of the reason people end up relapsing. No one likes to experience these types of negative feelings. The Choice Process approach to stopping can significantly reduce or eliminate those negative feelings. This time stopping can be a very positive experience as The Cycle of Deprivation is broken.

To illustrate what this cycle looks like, let's use the example of someone whose drinking has gotten out of control. We'll call him John. John's consequences and pain are beginning to cycle over and over daily. It begins to dawn on him, *"I don't like this. I have to stop drinking! This is getting crazy! I have got to stop doing this to myself and others!"* In addition, the people who are close to John begin noticing that things are going wrong, so they chime in, *"John, you've got to stop this, this is crazy! You can't drink!"* Every morning John wakes up to self - loathing and guilt. This day he vows to himself: *"Today is the day; I am going to not drink. I promise myself, I promise God – no more drinking!"* So, John musters up all the will-power he has, and he commits to stopping.

Now, some people are more disciplined than others, but for John as the day progresses he begins to waver under the pressure of his desire to use. He says to himself, *"Oh no, I can feel the urge starting. Oh man! I am really having a terrible urge but I am going to hold out here, because today is the day that I am going to stop!"* But the experience is very uncomfortable; in fact it is like torture, and John hates it. He wishes with all his might that the urge would just go away. John begins pacing the floor. He considers even calling a sponsor or a friend for support.

As time passes, the urge continues to build. This time John falls on his knees and prays, *"God, please just take these cravings away!"* At this point, John has "wished" his cravings away and he has tried to "pray them away," but the urge intensifies and he has become very, very uncomfortable. Nonetheless, John holds on.

Now, depending on the will-power of the individual, someone might hold on till 5 o'clock that day. They may hold on for one or two days or even a couple of weeks. The urge to drink, however, will continue to build and build. It is at this point that John and many of us want to cry out, desperate and discouraged, and say, *"Stop my addiction – are you kidding? It's awful! It feels like a punishment, like torture! I can't do this! I am too weak!"*

Finally, John's will-power is all used up. Not being able to hold on anymore, he finally gives in to the powerful urge. *"I just have to have a drink. Just one won't hurt. This will be the last time.*" So, John rushes out to the store to buy his "drink of choice." Now, bottle in hand he cracks it open. Mmmmm, the familiar scent of alcohol hits his olfactory senses. The anticipation of that well-known taste is overwhelming. The bottle tips back and he takes a long draw from the liquid within. Almost immediately John feels the familiar feeling of the alcohol washing over his brain as the "buzz" begins to form. As the effects of the alcohol take effect, that urge, which was at its pinnacle moments prior, finally goes away, and The Cycle of Deprivation is complete. Again we see how trying to stop feels like tortuous punishment and resuming using feels like a reward. This pattern may be repeated many times, and with each revolution the chains of addiction become stronger and it seems to the addicted that it is nearly impossible to break them. Often I will hear someone who is stuck in The Cycle of Deprivation say, *"I don't know how many times I quit, but I can abstain for only so long and then I'm back to using again."* What they don't understand, is that they are stuck in The Cycle of Deprivation. The good news is that this cycle can be broken.

This is where the power of CBT and the natural ability to rewire our brain comes into play. In this program we are going to change The Cycle of Deprivation around, so that stopping becomes the reward and the thought of using again is experienced as a punishment. This concept should seem logical to you. The idea of stopping as positive, and using again as negative, is indeed a useful concept, but that's only information. It's important that you proceed through all the steps of this program so that you can process the information on a gut level. Once you have experienced the steps outlined in this book, you will then be empowered to turn your desire to stop into a conviction of the heart, so when you say *"No"*, you really mean *"No."*

How exactly do I break The Cycle of Deprivation? One of the very unique aspects of this program is how we view the urge. Success depends on how we choose to frame our urges to use. If we view the urge as something negative - as something bad - then I am going to pull myself into The Cycle of Deprivation. But, the Choice Process helps us turn it around, and view the urge as a positive. The best way to counteract The Cycle of Deprivation and the negative view of the urge is by using the next phrase in the Choice Process: "I can use." This is a very important phrase, because it helps us to break the cycle. Remember how The Cycle of Deprivation works? I tell myself, or others tell me, that I CAN'T do something and I HAVE to stop; thereby making stopping a punishment and using again the reward. But, when I change my thinking around and say, *"You know, I CAN do this. No one can really stop me. If I really wanted to use, I know where to "score;" I know how to get what I need. The reality is I CAN!"* You see, "I can use" is a statement of truth, because the truth is, I can. When we say, "I can't use," it's not true. Why? Because the reality is that I can; I don't have to stop, and I always have a choice. The word "can't," as we will use it, means "CANNOT." It does not mean "wouldn't", "shouldn't" or "not supposed to." "Can't" means "can't." As soon as I say *"I can't..."* or someone says, *"You can't..."* they take away my choice – and we know now that we ALWAYS have a choice. Isn't that right?

I don't know about you, but I tend to have a bit of a rebellious streak inside of me. When people tell me I can't do something, it makes me want to do it all the more. I would imagine it's probably not much different with you. If someone tells you, *"You can't,"* those words tend to either incite rebellion or cause despair. Regardless, it's just not true. When I say to myself, *"I can't,"* I'm just lying to myself, because the truth of the matter is that I CAN. Take a moment and let that sink in. YOU CAN.

In just about any situation where you find yourself, you will be able to choose to do whatever you want to do:

Do you have a shopping addiction? When you max out a credit card you can just go get another credit card. What about alcohol? Consider the state where I live - Hawaii. Every store you go into has liquor on the shelves and many establishments will serve alcohol almost around the clock. You are going to be surrounded by it forever; you can only sequester yourself for so long. Are you addicted to online pornography? In today's society, there is internet wherever you go. Perhaps a loved one or someone holding you accountable decides to purchase password protected software on your device. But the truth is, if you want to gain access to the internet, you are going to discover an opportunity. Often, when someone has passwords on their computer or laptop to keep them from looking at pornography, they go through great pains of finding out what that password is, or they find a way around that password because the password is telling them *"you can't,"* and that is placing them smack-dab back in the middle of The Cycle of Deprivation. Too often, this kind of attempt to control ends up counter-productive.

Alright, the reality is, "I can use." I don't have to stop. Why? It is because YOU do have a choice in the matter. As we have discussed, you have choices in just about everything you do. For example, you made a choice to pick up this book and read it because you are capable of making that choice. You are responsible for educating yourself right now about the problem and solution to addiction. This morning when you woke up, you made a choice about the clothes that you are wearing right now, and so you are responsible for your appearance. In fact, in any situation in which you are capable of making a choice, you are not only responsible but you are in a position to gain control. For example, you are in control of where you are right now because you can make a choice to stay here or make a choice to leave. You see, 99% of the time you are capable of making these kinds of choices in 99% of your life. You ARE in control of your life. Except for one part, and that is when it comes to making choices about your addiction. Right now you are not capable of making those choices about your addiction, and that is why you are not in control.

To bring this area of your life under control, real change must happen from within. There must be an internal shift. External restraints, threats, ultimatums and attempts to "white knuckle it" will only be short-lived. In order for a person to make lasting changes, they have to come to the place where they decide for themselves. So, in this program we throw out the word "can't" because it takes away your power. "Can't" is a negative word, and the Choice Process approach is a positive alternative to that kind of counterproductive negativity. The truth of the matter is that you do have power. You CAN choose, and that is what the Choice Process helps you to discover.

In order for us to understand the power of deprivation and its negative force, let's consider the following illustration: Let's say that you win an all-expense paid trip to Disneyland with your family or perhaps with some close friends - picture that in your mind. For several weeks you make preparations; finally the big day comes, they fly you over to L.A., and you check into The Disneyland Hotel. The next morning all of you wake up excited and ready for lots of fun. Together, you walk through the gates of "The Magic Kingdom," and there you are, with your group, looking at the Disneyland map, and trying to decide what fun adventure to go to first. But then, I show up and with me are some deputies and a rolling jail cell – something like you might see circus animals locked in. I inform you that I'm sorry, but you will not be able to enjoy the park with everyone else. Instead, we will be locking you in the jail cell. So, I place you in the cell and, because it has wheels on it, we roll you around following behind your friends and family as they have a wonderful time. Picture yourself, locked inside the jail cell, feeling powerless and deprived. As your group comes out of the rides they are laughing and talking about how fun it was and what they experienced together, but you're sequestered away from all the fun.

Imagine yourself in this situation. What kinds of emotions might you be experiencing? How would you feel? What might you do? Most people in this situation would feel emotions like anger, frustration, sadness, a feeling of missing out, jealousy, or even shame ("I wonder what I did to deserve this?"). Some might say things like: *"Why me?" "This isn't fair!"* or *"I can't stand seeing everyone else have so much fun when I am locked away."* Some individuals may try to bargain their way out of the cell. Some may look around for a trap door, or try to pick the lock, or see if they can find another way out.

This is an example of deprivation. When you and I feel deprived from something that we want to do, we feel all sorts of negative emotions and feelings. The same is true when it comes to addressing addiction. If you feel that you CAN'T use, you're locking yourself into a "psychological jail cell" of your own making, where you will experience negative emotions and your mind will work overtime to figure out how to get around the "can't," So, when I am deprived, stopping becomes a punishment ("I can't") and using again becomes a reward. This endless cycle is like a flushing toilet, it sends the enslaved person deeper and deeper into the sewer of their addiction.

(Review your "list of consequences" on the previous page for confirmation of this negative cycle.)

God has made us creatures that have the freedom of choice. In the Old Testament of The Bible, Joshua stood before the Hebrew people and laid out their options: *"But if serving the LORD seems undesirable to you, then choose for yourselves this day whom you will serve..."*[6] God has created and made us creatures of free will. He knows that we can choose to follow Him or we can choose to not follow Him. You cannot control people and say, *"You can't do this!"* because they can. This is a VERY important concept for us to understand. One of the major goals of this program is to teach you a choice-making process that will accomplish two things: First of all, when you say *"No,"* you will really mean it, and secondly, you will actually feel good about saying *"No."* If saying *"no"* makes you feel good, then what are you going to say? *"No!"* That's where the consistency comes into play. If you can make the positive choice to say *"no"* and it feels good, that's how you will get control in the long run.

By the way, living under the banner of "can't" burdens others as well. Please don't buy into the whole idea of, *"I am not a drinker anymore so let's get rid of all the alcohol in the house"* – I am not for that at all, that's

---

[6] Joshua 24:15a NIV

setting yourself up for deprivation. That's making you into a "bubble boy" or "bubble girl" who relies on others to keep them clean and sober by creating a sequestered and sterile environment.

Saying "I can" doesn't mean that you will. Instead, it breaks up feelings of deprivation and empowers a person to make the choices that they desire. Saying *"I can use"* gives you the power.

Figure it out

· I _____ use   (this statement helps break the Cycle of Deprivation)

Why are "I can't use" and "I have to stop," not true? – Because the reality is you can. You don't have to stop. You have a choice.

➢ When you say that you "can't" engage in the behavior, you are really lying to yourself (because you can.)

➢ When you say you "can't" you take away your _____, and you always have a choice, you are in control of your decisions.

➤ When you say that you "can't" you set yourself up for The Cycle of _____ where stopping becomes punishment and using becomes the reward

List 5 common symptoms of deprivation

a. _____   b. _____

c. _____   d. _____

e. _____   f. _____

g. _____   h. _____

Saying "I can't" locks you into a psychological jail cell of your own creation.

It's time to grab your token and recite your Choice Process. Read it out loud several times:

"I want to use, I can use, however once and it's over. So in this moment I choose to accept temporary discomfort so I can get my benefits

Chapter 7
"However, once and it's over..."
Accepting the reality of addiction

"However, once and it's over." What is over? Your benefits: happiness, peace, financial security, healthy relationships, self-respect, attainable present and future goals, ability to do what you love, safety for you and others, a sense of well-being, no more guilt or fear, basically the life you dream of. All the benefits that you have worked so hard to achieve in remaining clean and sober can be thrown out with one drink or one hit; a single decision, made in a moment of desperation and weakness, to go back for "one last time." If I've been enjoying abstinence for a particular period of time, and then all of a sudden I engage in my addictive behavior again, all of those benefits of abstinence are out the window and I will slip once again into the slimy pit of addiction.

Up to this point, we have placed all types of addictions together in one big lump. However, we now have to make some distinctions. There are some things we can become addicted to that we actually need: i.e. food, exercise or shopping. You can't stop eating. You should have some form of exercise and we know everyone has to take a trip to the store from time to time.

It was Aristotle who said, *"Seek moderation in all things."*[7] The problem is that there are certain substances and addictions where moderation is not realistic. If a drug is illegal or a person wanting to drink is underage, there really isn't a "moderate" use that lines up with the law. Depending on the moral code and value system you have submitted to, there is no moderation when it comes to pornography. However, with legal substances and amoral behaviors, one can partake "in moderation." So, for instance, I can enjoy a scrumptious dessert, have a good workout session, take advantage of a sale at my local department store, and even drink alcohol moderately (if I am of legal age).

Often an individual goes through treatment and chooses to stop abusing illegal substances like: crack cocaine, heroin, meth, and medication without a prescription. Choosing to turn their back on any of these substances will result in no use at all – if they want to get their benefits. One can still choose to use, but they would risk not only returning to their addictive ways, but also incarceration and legal troubles. If your motivation to get clean and sober includes happiness, peace, and joy, then

---

[7] Aristotle, Doctrine of The Mean, Nicomachean Ethics

losing your freedom is a sure-fire way to sabotage all you are working towards.

When it comes to an illegal substance or immoral behavior, there is no middle ground – no moderation. These are issues of right and wrong or black and white. The challenge for some is the areas of life where moderation CAN be a reality. If you have a food addiction, you still have to eat. If you have a shopping addiction, you will still have to shop. If your particular addiction is drinking alcohol, you are looking out at a world where there are a lot of people who choose to drink moderately. Let's once again turn to problem drinking or alcoholism to understand what "once and it's over" is all about.

I think alcohol is a gift from God. The problem isn't the actual substance; the problem is that people misuse the substance. For some of us, moderation is not a reality. Think of a light switch on a wall. It's either off or on – no middle ground. That's the way it is when I drink. If I drink one, I want ten. I marvel at my wife. She will buy a bottle of wine, have one glass, cork the bottle and not drink any more for weeks. She has a "take-it-or-leave-it" attitude towards drinking. My wife and millions of drinkers like her, practice moderation when it comes to their drinking choices. But for me, I have come to the realization that moderation is not my reality.

Out of all the phrases in the Choice Process this is often the hardest one for many to accept. *"You mean I will never be able to drink again – not even one beer at New Year's or a glass of wine on my anniversary?"* Look, you can do whatever you want. It's your program. However, if you truly are addicted, you have crossed the "moderation line" and there is no going back. Remember, there are six separate phrases that make up the Choice Process. The first three are statements of truth. This third statement sums up the truth for people enslaved in addiction. Moderation may not be your reality but if that's the case, your mind must come to accept that truth – to embrace it.

For problem drinkers and alcoholics, the war started years ago when cutting down and cutting back were desperate attempts to return to moderation. By limiting drinks or creating little rules like, "only at special occasions," we made futile attempts to return to drinking moderately—*"Hey, other people can do it why not me?"* For the true addict, moderation doesn't work. But that information is hard to take. Getting high can be like a friend. Once again, consider alcohol: If I am happy, I want a drink. If I am sad, I want a drink. If I am celebrating, I want a drink. If I am grieving, I want a drink. If I am tired,

I want a drink. If I am energetic, I want a drink. Get the picture?

Several years ago, rock and roll artist George Thorogood and The Destroyers released a song entitled "I Drink Alone".[8] The song spoke directly to those addicted to alcohol. Mr. Thorogood's description of an intimate relationship between an isolated drinker and the various brands of alcohol that had become his "friends," struck a chord for those who have experienced a similar bond. If you have never heard the song I encourage you to find it on the internet and take a listen. It's no wonder that "once and it's over" is such a hard concept to swallow, when a long standing "friendship" has come to an end.

How does the phrase, "However, once and it's over" strike you? Is it hard to accept? I invite you to "grieve" your fantasy of moderation. Grieving moderation means I accept the fact that I'm not a moderate person and I let the idea of moderation in my life die. Elisabeth Kübler-Ross, in her 1969 book "On Death and Dying", wrote about 5 stages of grief. Since that writing, others have added to her observations, creating the popular notion of seven different "stages" of grief. A grief counselor would tell you that each person who grieves does not necessarily go through all seven stages, nor do they sequentially go

---

8   From the album, "Maverick" Released: 1985 George Thorogood and The Destroyers

from one to another in order. However, there is a commonality to grief, and it can be helpful for those who are grieving a loss to understand what is happening to them. I have taken the popular seven stages and modified them to fit the Choice Process understanding of "grieving moderation."

7 Stages of Grief
"Mourning Moderation"

· **Stage One - Shock or Disbelief**

You mean I can't ever drink (or use) again? That is crazy! Let's not get too radical and extreme. I don't want to go overboard with this treatment thing. Certainly, after I have learned my lesson, I can return to moderation.

· **Stage Two - Denial**

Abstinence is just not my reality. This can't be happening to me. It's not THAT bad. I can handle this. I may have a problem, but at least I don't drink or use like the bum who is living under the bridge.

- **Stage Three - Anger**

Why me? I can't believe this! This isn't fair! Don't tell me what to do!

- **Stage Four - Bargaining**

Well, if I go through this treatment and really do well, can I return back to "just once in a while?" When a lot of time has passed and I have "been really good," then certainly I should be able to return to using on special occasions, just weekends, or only on birthdays or holidays. Surely, that must be okay.

- **Stage Five - Guilt**

If I give up partying I will let my friends down. My spouse will be mad because they like to party with me. I will be a drag. No one will like me. They will consider me a "downer." They won't want me to be around them because I'll prohibit them from having a good time.

- **Stage Six - Depression**

  I feel sad about the thought of not drinking socially, not having my "friend" with me (substance). I feel lonely. I feel down.

- **Stage Seven - Acceptance and Hope**

  I finally accept the fact that "I am not a moderate person – moderation is not my reality." As much as I would like it to be, I have come to accept that reality. I finally have embraced the New Me. The New Me who does not drink or use drugs. I like the New Me. I now walk with my head up, living in confidence and hope.

You see, "once and it's over" relates to a mourning process, not only for you, but sometimes your spouse or friend may have to mourn your moderation as well. Back when my wife and I were dating, part of the fun we had is when we would go to the local pizza parlor where you could order a pitcher of beer with your pizza. We would sit, talk and laugh for hours. Do you remember the "benefits of using" list you created earlier? Perhaps you noticed that alcohol "loosens the tongue;" you laugh, you share, the conversation flows. Later on, when I came to the realization that drinking was a problem for me, I had to mourn the fact that I was not able to be moderate in order to responsibly enjoy outings such as these. My decision to become abstinent not only affected me, but it affected my wife as well. Accepting the fact that you are not a moderate person is imperative. When you embrace the "New Me," you can look around and see other people being moderate and not experience resentment.

"However, once and it's over" can be further clarified with what I call "The Train Illustration." Once again, I will use alcohol addiction for the purposes of this analogy. Imagine your addiction was illustrated by a train ride across the continental United States. The train ride begins in Los Angeles – representing when you took your first drink, and it ends in New York City – which would represent death by cirrhosis of the liver. Back in L.A., at the beginning of your journey, you may have chosen to drink in moderation; perhaps you would have only a beer or two. But as time went by, your drinking escalated. A couple of beers turned into a six pack, then binge drinking and eventually into a daily habit that far exceeded what anyone would regard as moderate.

Finally, after the pain and consequences of drinking took their toll you decided to call it quits and you get off the train. We will say that this departure happened in Texas – around the middle of the U.S. After enjoying abstinence for a while, maybe even a treatment program of some sort, you begin to contemplate the idea of drinking again. It's your plan to return to the "L.A. days of drinking." After a great deal of internal deliberation (which includes a whole lot of rationalizing and justifying) you start drinking again. *"Ahh!" you say. "This time will be different. I have learned my lesson. I will only drink moderately from now on."* The reality is this: Within a week you will return to the "Texas" amount you were drinking when you stopped and you will escalate from there towards New York City, increasing your alcohol intake even more than when you quit at Texas.

For many people who have struggled with addiction for years, this illustration makes complete sense. On a personal note, I took my first drink at age 13 and my own personal journey with drugs and alcohol lasted a little over 20 years. Along the way I "got off at Texas" and went to an Alcoholics Anonymous program. The lady who ran the program was wonderful and I made lots of good friends and had terrific support. I was abstinent for about 4 years. However, during that 4-year period I was pining away to drink again: *"Life was so much more fun when I was drinking. I think I have learned my lesson. I am much stronger now."*

And then, one particular Christmas Eve, I convinced myself I was going to be fine. *"One little drink is not going to hurt me."* I rationalized. During that deliberation period I started to think back to when I first started on my own "train ride." I remembered the time when I drank one or two beers and everything WAS fine, so I convinced myself that Christmas Eve would be my "all aboard!" ticket once again. Guess what? It wasn't a week or two until my drinking returned to "Texas" levels and escalated from there. Today I am grateful that I got off the train for good before I hit the East Coast.

In the world of treatment and rehab, there is a statement that can be controversial. That statement is: "Relapse is part of recovery." Some counselors don't want to ever say it, because they feel it gives their client "permission" to jump "off the wagon" and drink again. *"After all, since relapse is part of recovery then it looks like I will need to relapse a few times... pour me another one Charlie!"* But that is not how I look at the statement. I believe that "relapse IS part of recovery" and it is a true statement. Addicts have very hard heads. They rationalize, justify, and convince themselves, and others, that *"they can quit any time they want to."* And because of this propensity to keep "trying to be moderate," they will bang their head against the wall over and over and over again.

71

This is where "relapse is part of recovery" rings true. An addict has to experiment with the whole idea that I can "handle it." *"Oh, I've learned my lesson now; I can be moderate." "I am only going to use my credit cards for online purchasing."* or *"I am only going to use the slot machines at the airport in Las Vegas."* Your mind will concoct these types of excuses that you now have a handle on your addiction. A person usually must try it for themselves before they are finally convinced, *"This ain't gonna work."* You can try to return to L.A., but the train is leaving and it's heading towards New York.   *"All aboard!!?"*

I love the way one of my clients put it when he was reviewing his own journey towards relapse. He said, *"I guess I am not done with my research."* I love that line. Now, when one of my clients starts the program and they are doing great, but then choose to use, they will come back to see me with "their tail between their legs," realizing the futility of returning to their addiction. I will say to them, *"Looks like you needed to do some more research"* and then reassure them that they are still on the right path. Returning to using can be a disappointment, but we continue to press forward.

"However, once and it's over." This is the third of three truth statements. Complete the assignments for this chapter and we will move to the first of the three declarative statements that complete our Choice Process.

Figure it

· However, once and its _____

(This phrase helps you to become aware of false confidence)

What is over? _____

What does this phrase mean to you?

_____

_____

_____

What does your "train ride" look like for you? (Your history of substance abuse – beginning till now)

_____

_____

_____

_____

_____

_____

Describe your "L.A." (How substance abuse got started: experimentation, sneaking drinks, etc.)

_____

_____

_____

_____

_____

_____

Describe what your addiction looked like when you got off the train

_____

_____

_____

It's time to grab your token and recite your Choice Process. Read it out loud several times:

"I want to use, I can use, however once and it's over. So in this moment I choose to accept temporary discomfort so I can get my benefits."

Chapter 8
"So in this moment..."
Allow me to introduce you to your
"Junkie Mind."

A popular slogan in Alcoholics Anonymous is "One Day at a Time." This timeless wisdom has, no doubt, guided a great many people through their first days and weeks of recovery. With the Choice Process type of approach, we acknowledge that within one day there are 24 hours and within those 24 hours are 1,440 separate minutes. For someone struggling with strong urges, they may face temptation several times in one day. So, that is why part of the Choice Process phraseology is the following declaration: "So in this moment..."

Early on in recovery, it is not uncommon for an individual to start worrying and obsessing about what will happen in the future. *"I am clean and sober now, but what about the office Christmas party coming up? Everyone will be drinking and what if they hand me a martini?"* Or, *"I am feeling strong today, but in two weeks, my wife and kids will be traveling to her mom's house, and I will be all alone for a few days."* Or, *"I worry about having that much freedom."* Or, *"I seem fine when I am in my routine here at home, but soon, my work will be sending me all over the country on various business trips. What if I slip up?"*

Let me introduce you to the concept of "The Junkie Mind." I'm sure that you have seen a cartoon where one of the characters is going through some kind of internal struggle, and in order to illustrate their dilemma, the cartoonists have drawn an angel on one shoulder and the devil on the other. Both the angel and the devil are taking turns speaking into the character's ear and trying to convince them their particular argument is the best.

With that visual in mind, you will have an idea of the concept of your Junkie Mind. Your Junkie Mind is really you, or that part of you that will do anything to get you to use again. The Junkie Mind is very, very cunning and smart, and is always working out the future. I want you to visualize your Junkie Mind. Some people see him or her as drug "junkie": disheveled, dirty, sweating and needing a fix. I like to picture him as a slick lawyer, dressed up wearing an expensive three piece suit.

You are in a chess match with your Junkie Mind. For those of you who play the game of chess you know that as you are contemplating your next move, it's not just that particular move that counts. In order to be a good chess player, you need to anticipate three moves ahead.

You need to think through what your opponent is going to do once you make your move, and then have a well thought out strategy that will counter their next one. Your Junkie Mind is always working in the future, and is scheming how they can get you back to using again. If you are not three steps ahead of your Junkie Mind, you will fall prey to his or her schemes.

Part of being aware of the Junkie Mind is to know the arguments. The Junkie Mind whispers phrases like these into your ear:

"You've been such a good boy (or girl). You deserve a treat."

"Just once won't hurt."

"No one will find out, you can cover your tracks."

"It's been such a long time; you have learned your lesson. You will be okay."

I talk to people all the time that have stopped their addiction and had a long stretch of enjoying their freedom. But after months, or even years, they went back, used, and became enslaved all over again. In every case it's because they listened to their Junkie Mind. Your Junkie Mind is lying in wait, looking for the opportunity to pounce. What is your Junkie Mind saying to you?

Learn to have a conversation with your Junkie Mind and use the various phrases of the Choice Process as part of your dialogue. For example:

Junkie Mind: *"It's been a long time since you've had a drink. Just one won't hurt."*

Your reply: *"Yes, Junkie Mind, you are right. It has been a long time, but the truth is - once and it's over."*

Junkie Mind: *"But you've been so good! You deserve a treat."*

Your reply: *"You're right, I do deserve a treat. I want to drink and I can, but getting enslaved again is not who I want to be."*

Junkie Mind: *"Just this once. No one will know."*

Your reply: *"I will know. Thanks for the offer, but in this moment I will choose temporary discomfort so I can get my benefits."*

The phrase "So in this moment..." will remind you that the Junkie Mind is always working out in the future, planning and scheming your next high or addiction experience. Your Junkie Mind wants you to obsess about the future so that he/she can panic you back to using again. For example, let's say it's November and you stop drinking. The Junkie Mind starts working you over about the future. *"What about the family vacation during Thanksgiving?"* *"What about your office Christmas party?" "What about New Years Eve – you ALWAYS drink on New Years!"* If you start listening to your Junkie Mind the panic will rise up and you will say, *"Oh forget it. What's the use!"* and then you will take another drink and the Junkie Mind has won, because you've sabotaged yourself by not <u>staying in the present</u>. The reason you used is not because "in this moment" was a problem, right now was just fine. The reason you used was because your Junkie Mind got you into the future and you decided you knew what the future would bring, what was going to happen and became overwhelmed.

Imagine your thoughts are like a helium balloon that is attached to a very long string. As your thoughts drift out to the future, I want you to pull on that string and bring the balloon down; this will bring your thoughts back into the present. You cannot control what happens in the future, so there is no use obsessing and worrying about it. The only moment that you have control over is THIS moment, right now. Everything that you hope might happen, or even plan to do in the future, is really just a suggested reality. If you find yourself out in the future, exercise the skill of bringing yourself back into the moment. This is very important. Once you develop this skill, it will come naturally over time.

Here's another illustration that may help: Let's say that I talked to my wife and we decide we're going to have a date this Friday night and go to the movies to see a new release. That's a suggested reality. Truly, anything can happen between now and the moment that date happens that would change our plans. Somebody could get sick; we could have another engagement that comes up that we have to attend, or the car could break down on the way to the theater. The only time that our plan will become a reality is when we actually step into the movie theatre and watch the movie. The point here is the only time you really have control, is "in this moment."

Take some time and complete the following "figure it" exercises. Learn to identify the unique chatter of your Junkie Mind and to stay present in the moment.

Figure it out

· So, in this _____

(This phrase helps you become aware of self-sabotage)

Fact: you only have control over this moment.

What is your "Junkie Mind?"

_____

_____

Why is "getting out in the future", when it comes to stopping, a pitfall?

_____

_____

What does your Junkie Mind say to you? What are some of his/her favorite arguments?

_____

_____

It's time to grab your token and recite your Choice Process. Read it out loud several times:

"I want to use, I can use, however once and it's over. So in this moment I choose to accept temporary discomfort so I can get my benefits

81

Chapter 9
"I choose to accept temporary discomfort..."
The life skill of delayed gratification

In 1972, psychologist Walter Mischel of Stanford University conducted what is now known as "The Marshmallow Experiment." Mischel ran his experiment on the campus of the university where there was a daycare center. In this daycare center they set up a room with a "two way mirror," so that Mishel and his researchers could observe the children without their knowledge. In the experiment, various sweets that included a single marshmallow were placed in front of young children, around the age of four, by their teacher. The teacher then explained that they had to leave the room for a moment. The children were told that they could eat the marshmallow if they wanted to; however, if they waited until the teacher returned they could get two more. Some children gobbled the tasty treat almost immediately. Others fidgeted in their seats, tortured by the decision to eat or not to eat. Some of the children nibbled a little on the snack and then returned the uneaten portion to the plate in such a way that the part they ate was not showing.

Many of the kids successfully waited and were able to receive the promised two more marshmallows in return.

Over 600 children participated in this original experiment, which was designed to identify the mental processes that allowed some people to delay gratification, while others simply surrendered. It was really the follow up research that made the most waves in the psychology community. Nearly ten years later, Mischel did a follow up study of these children – most of them now in high school. Once Mischel began analyzing the results, he noticed that the children who didn't seem to possess the life skill of delayed gratification and ate the marshmallow right away, seemed more likely to have behavioral problems, both in school and at home. They got lower S.A.T. scores. They struggled in stressful situations, often had trouble paying attention, and found it difficult to maintain friendships. The children who could wait fifteen minutes had an S.A.T. score that was, on average, two hundred and ten points higher than that of the kid who could wait only thirty seconds.[9]

"I choose to accept temporary discomfort" is a phrase that describes the life skill of delayed gratification. If you have it, you will do well in life. If you don't have it, then the skill needs to be developed. We live in a culture

---

[9] Condé Nast publishers. The New Yorker online magazine

and society that doesn't always promote this skill. Everything from instant popcorn in microwaves, to high speed internet, to 'buy it now with one click' on your credit card, feeds the path of least resistance and develops the craving for instant gratification rather than delaying our desires.

When it comes to treating addiction, the "temporary discomfort" is that of the urge to use. Because the urge to use can be mentally and physically uncomfortable, one can understandably feel "hatred" towards their urge. Why is the addiction urge perceived as negative? Because, it makes you feel uncomfortable, you see no value in the urge. We have conditioned ourselves over time to put a negative value on the urge, when in actuality; an urge is just that – an urge. You may try to "pray" it away or "wish" it away - it still remains with you.

When addiction happens, it is because we have spent months or even years training our body to physiologically react to a particular behavior. Those thoughts and feelings are not going to disappear overnight. This is why we are in the process of rewiring our thought patterns. They are a natural part of the choices we have made and what has gotten us to the point where we now are. We loath the urges and curse them and pray that God will take them away, but we have created them. This is our own fault. Instead of wasting time wishing they were gone, change how you think. You can rewire your thought process and the experience will turn from negative to positive.

Let's suppose we have a weekend binge drinker and its Monday morning. He is not experiencing an urge because it is only Monday, so his urge is repressed, buried in the subconscious mind. But as Friday night approaches, the urge climbs slowly from the subconscious, into awareness, and then becomes more and more intense. When the urge reaches its peak, what does he do? He uses. What does he accomplish by using? The urge goes away. But it doesn't go away forever; it's still there just waiting to come out again. It may stay away for a few hours, a day, maybe even a few days or a week, but sooner or later, "urge" will meet "opportunity" and the binge begins again. This is a picture of addiction.

Some approaches say, *"Okay, we see what the problem is – it's this urge."* They tell you things like, *"Stay away from your drinking friends. Go to meetings every day. Stay away from any place where you might 'trigger.' Change your lifestyle."* You may have tried these approaches and they didn't really work. It's because, no matter what you do, that urge still comes out. The problem is not your environment - the problem is inside of you. This is one of the most consistent realities in your life and it has been for some time. That urge is not just going to dry up and blow away. So, the key here is not to hide from reality by trying to hide from the urge. When was the last time you accomplished anything by running from it? The key here is to learn to deal with reality. This program is designed to teach you how to deal with that urge so you don't fear it. In fact, you use the energy of it to get what you want. That's how you gain control.

Often times someone battling with their urges develop a simple formula in their thinking: "urge = wrong, relief = right." In other words, if I feel the discomfort of the urge, something must be "wrong." When I use again the urge goes away so using must be "right." It's easy to see how this kind of thinking can develop. Consider the urge of thirst or a hunger pang. When our body is low on calories and hydration we become physically uncomfortable. This is our body's natural way to tell us to eat or drink. If we didn't we would eventually die. So, the uncomfortable feeling of thirst or hunger tells us something is wrong. When we eat or drink the feeling goes away and we feel "right" again. With addiction, our body has come to "need" the substance. We have addicted ourselves to the natural brain chemicals that are released when we use. This is both a physical addiction and a psychological addiction. Together, the urge to use is uncomfortable and we loathe it.

So, how can you learn to "accept" the urge? The key to gaining control is learning to accept the urge and making a choice about it. You are much more likely to accept something positive than negative. I am going to teach you how to do this. Using CBT and the Choice Process, we are going to change the formula. Instead of "urge = wrong, relief = right," we will change our mindset about the urge so that it now symbolizes to us that we ARE getting what we want – our benefits.

How one can view discomfort in a positive way? We do this by retraining our minds to accept the discomfort as a positive sign that we are getting our benefits. The urge signals to you that you now have a chance to "work" so you can gain control. If you are trying to deal with your addiction problem, the only time you can learn control is when you are facing an urge. This gives you an opportunity. Seems counter-intuitive doesn't it? Consider the following illustration that might help shed some light on this CBT process of changing your thoughts.

Have you ever had a deep tissue massage? My wife enjoys having them often. She tells me that when she is on the table the pain can be excruciating at times. As the masseuse uses her fingers, hands, and even her elbows to push deep into the knotted muscles, she will wince in pain. Why would she put up with such discomfort? To get her benefits. She tells me that when she is on the table the pain "hurts so good," because she knows when she walks out the door she will feel like a million bucks. As a rational adult, she can make a decision about how she views such discomfort. If we put a 4 year old child on the massage table, they will cry out in fear and pain, wondering why someone would be so mean to hurt them. As an adult, we can look at the pain rationally and place a different value on it - a positive outlook.

Let's say you wake up today and it's raining. Is the rain bad or good? It depends on the value you place on the rainy day. If you had big plans for a sunny day at the beach then you might think the rain was bad. If you just planted a garden that needed to be watered or wanted to curl up with a good book, you might think the rain was good. It all depends on how you choose to think about it.

An urge is not a positive or negative thing in itself; it has no inherent value. The urge is something that you can choose to place a value on. It's for you to decide whether this urge is a good or bad thing. The urge itself is just a mental impulse; it's just a tiny, bouncing electrical signal in your brain. It cannot have any inherent value. You give it value.

Think about your addiction right now. Do you have an urge to use? Suppose that you say *"no"* you are not having an urge to use at this moment. So, as of right now, you have no urge to use. Is it hard for you NOT to use? No, it's not a problem now; in fact, you might not even feel addicted right now. However, we know that sooner or later that urge to use will be there, and then will it be hard for you NOT to use? Of course! Yes, this is when it gets difficult. So, when is using a problem for you? When you are having an urge or not having an urge? Of course, it's when you are having the urge. Therefore, given the fact that the only time you can deal with a problem is when it exists, and the only time using is a problem is when you have an urge; the urge can be your friend.

Since you have chosen this time to address your addiction, and to live with a focus on attaining your benefits, it's time for you to change your thought process concerning your urges. Now we think this: URGE = OPPORTUNITY. Each time you experience an urge you are presented with the opportunity to gain control over your problem. Each time you choose your benefits, you give yourself more strength, and your addiction less strength. This thinking is probably completely opposite from everything you have ever told yourself, and so we need to retrain your thinking about the urge. It's very important that you start some active, serious conversation with yourself about what this urge is all about. So, when you experience an urge just ask yourself, *"Is this urge good or bad?"* Then tell yourself that it's good. Why? Because, it is your opportunity to deal with your addiction – to gain control. It's your opportunity to get all the things on your list of benefits that you created earlier. Seize the experience of the urge as an opportunity to deal with the problem.

You see, "I can choose to accept temporary discomfort" because it represents that I am going to get what I want – the benefits of sobriety. Being sober brings with it a whole slew of benefits. We will talk more about this in the next chapter. Why would we want to put up with the discomfort of the urge? ANSWER: To get our benefits!

Remember the Cycle of Deprivation that was discussed in chapter 6? The urge builds and builds and we feel as if we are being deprived of something that we desperately need. Then we use, and the urge goes away. So, stopping is regarded as a punishment and using again as a reward. Consider this: <u>As long as my urge is there it means that I am not using</u>. So, my urge should be considered a badge of honor, which means I'm doing well and getting my benefits.

I live in a town that is near two military bases. From time to time I will see those in the armed forces in their dress uniforms. Many of these brave soldiers wear a series of colored rectangles over their chest area. Each one represents a medal that they have earned. As a civilian, all I see are colored ribbons and rectangular bars; however, on occasion I have pointed to one of the awards and asked a military friend what their badge means. Always, with pride, the soldier will launch into a story of how they earned it, relishing their accomplishment and enjoying the reward of being able to share their story even though earning the badge usually involved some level of pain and discomfort that they had to endure.

An urge is just an urge, and when it comes to our thinking about the urge, you can write your own ticket. If I choose to regard the urge as positive, I do so because it symbolizes that I'm getting what I want; then the urge becomes a good thing. If I decide that the urge is terrible and awful and horrendous, then I will not learn to accept it. If I see the urge as my "badge of honor," because I am not using, I am getting my benefits and the urge can be experienced much more positively.

And remember, it's only TEMPORARY discomfort. Over time the urge will subside and even disappear all together in some cases. Our phrase is "I choose to accept temporary discomfort." The operative word here is "temporary." This is a very important word – a word that leads to hope and perseverance. If you are not willing to put up with discomfort, then you are not willing to do the work necessary to stop addiction. When someone begins to become abstinent, urges are going to be strong. This is the point in time when we repeat the Choice Process over and over and over during the day. As we say it over and over, we are facing these urges head on. The good news is this: As you experience success in your abstinence, those urges will begin to subside over time, and you will be simultaneously rewiring your brain and re-shaping your physiology. This brain plasticity is a God given built-in mechanism for change. The discomfort that you initially feel is not going to be of the same intensity and level for the rest of your life. If you refuse to accept your urges you will be trying to repress, or push the urges out of your mind. When this happens, you are not dealing with the problem or dealing with reality. As a result of this refusal to accept the urge, you run the danger of relapse.

You and I hang on to the things we regard as positive in our lives. If something is negative, you might put up with it for a while, but you will not embrace it forever. We "choose to accept" the temporary discomfort because we understand that it's the pathway to getting the life, and benefits we desire. Make the choice to accept the discomfort. It is only temporary. If you make the choice to reject your discomfort, and you start using again - how long could that last?   ANSWER: A lifetime of enslavement.

Figure it out

- I   choose   to   _____   temporary _____

(This phrase helps the stopping process positive instead of negative)

Why is the addiction urge perceived as a negative?

How can you learn to "accept" the urge? -

How one can view discomfort in a positive way?

It's time to grab your token and recite your Choice Process. Read it out loud several times:

"I want to use, I can use, however once and it's over. So in this moment I choose to accept temporary discomfort so I can get my benefits.

Chapter 10

"So I can get my benefits..."

The engine that drives your sobriety for life

Go back and look at your "Benefit List" that you created at the end of chapter two. If you were thorough, the list should be very long. Each of your benefits could be put into various categories:

Relational benefits – When I am not using I am more mentally, emotionally and physically available to those I love. Addiction keeps me guarded and isolated. I might become moody or ugly in my interactions. Sometimes substance abuse might cause you to feel euphoric and "happy." You may feel like you are the life of the party or a great conversationalist, but others around you sense something is wrong. People know when connection is authentic or when it is fabricated. Being free from addiction creates a "clear head" and a greater ability to be a better friend, lover, spouse, employee or parent.

Health benefits – The more addicted a person becomes, the more energy they will need to put towards keeping their life manageable. Many times addicts go to great lengths to "cover their tracks" so that others don't find out the true nature of their problem. This constant vigil to "not get caught" is stressful. Many times people don't realize that they live their life at a chronic, low level of anxiety, for fear that others will find out what REALLY is going on in the back room, during the car ride home, at the office or at night when everyone else is asleep.

Many of our soldiers who come back from war-torn areas come home with Post Traumatic Stress Disorder. PTSD can be caused by living with a low level of anxiety for a long period of time. For instance, let's say I am deployed downrange and I am in a unit that goes out on daily patrol in the town and countryside where I am stationed. Every day, part of that patrol is to go under a bridge overpass. Because of our training, we know that bridges are favorite targets for the enemy to place I.E.D bombs (improvised explosive device). Every day of our one year deployment we dread the bridge overpass patrol. Our bodies tense up, our fears rise then fall. We learn to live with the stress.

Finally your deployment is over, now you can return home and get on with "life as normal." But shortly after you return, you take a drive with the family on the freeway and up ahead you see an overpass. Guess what comes flooding back? Your body goes into overdrive with all those feelings of going under that bridge on patrol. You tense up, and feel like you are going to have a panic attack. This is an example of what it can be like to suffer with PTSD.

Those who are enslaved by addictive behavior learn to live with a low-level stress that can affect them emotionally, spiritually, mentally and physically. Consider what happens to heavy drinkers when they finally stop. If you drink heavily every day and then you stop, especially for the first week, you will probably notice that you have very vivid dreams. Many drinkers claim that alcohol helps them to go to sleep. It actually can help you to drift off to sleep at first; however, you will sleep fitfully and never slip into that all important Stage 4, REM sleep that the body needs to repair itself, to dream, to be healthy.

Financial benefits – People will do almost anything to feed their addiction. Bank accounts can be drained, savings can be squandered and a paycheck may disappear overnight. Some people sadly resort to "borrowing" money from friends and loved ones, but the repayment plan never seems to materialize. I live in Hawaii, and there are establishments in the downtown area where a single drink can run as high as $20. Being released from the slavery of addiction frees up your finances so you can do something nice for your kids, save for the future, or help someone in need.

Self Image benefits – It's no fun to self-loathe. Self-loathing is when you beat yourself up after "once again" returning to your addictive behavior. Often times, this happens first thing in the morning. You wake up, perhaps with a hangover or an empty pocketbook. Immediately your mind drifts to the evening before, and you are reminded of how you once again engaged in the very behavior you swore off the previous morning. It's hard to feel good about yourself if you are violating your own value system! What a wonderful feeling it is to wake up and know that you are clear headed, you are productive, and you are able to be emotionally present with those you love.

Spiritual Benefits – If you are a faith based person who believes in God, then you know what I am talking about. You value your relationship with God, but you know that when you are doing the wrong thing, it puts a wedge between you and your Creator. Freedom from addiction once again allows you to worship, pray, and enjoy God's presence. The fact of the matter is God has ALWAYS been there for you; it was you who distanced yourself. If you are a Believer in God, I invite you to make the Choice Process into a prayer. Invite Him into the moment each time you experience an urge. He is there anyway and He knows what you are going through. Let's say you are feeling a strong urge to drink, here's how it's done: *"Father, I want to take a drink right now and I can – because you have given me free will. However, I realize that if I do take the drink – it's over. So, in this moment I am going to make the choice to accept the temporary discomfort of the urge so I can get my benefits. And one of my benefits is enjoying talking to you. Thank you for being there with me in this moment."*

The above benefit categories are just the tip of the iceberg, and represent hundreds of good things that can be enjoyed when you are released from the bondage of addiction. Think back to chapter two when we covered incentive. This is your time in life to be "selfish." Make sure that your benefits are for you; rejoice and embrace them. It's true, when you are free other people in your life will benefit, but that's the "trickledown effect" of your choice to stop.

Your benefit package will help you to embrace what I call the "New Me." How do I embrace the "New Me?" When we rewire our brain to embrace the benefits of abstinence the reward switches from using to not using. Therefore, the choice to be abstinent comes from within and has long-lasting results. Often times, people will use a tremendous amount of will-power to stop their addictive behavior, but they haven't really done the internal work inside. They may pine away for "the good old days" when they used to party, while not actively using, but never fully embracing their sobriety. To embrace the "New Me" means: I like myself sober, not using, and not engaging in destructive behavior. When I think about the "Old Me," I have compassion, but not a fondness for who I was because under the throes of addiction I am not the person I want to be, and I don't want to be that person ever again.

Saying the Choice Process is not a mantra. These are not "magic words" that will make your urge disappear. The words and phrases of the Choice Process will remind you of the backbone of this program and your commitment to getting what you want out of life. But saying the phrases over and over again can become monotonous if you are not careful. Here is how you can keep it fresh. Each time you say your Choice Process, select a different benefit. When you say the last line, "I choose to accept temporary discomfort so I can get my benefits," pick a different benefit from your list you made in chapter two and spend a few seconds meditating on how much you enjoy having that particular benefit now that you are not using. For example, let's say one of your benefits is your relationship with your spouse that is no longer compromised because of your addiction. Then at the end of your Choice Process, "...so I can get my benefits," you then think to yourself, *"And one of my benefits is enjoying my spouse. I feel much closer to him or her now that I am not hiding or lying or isolating myself in order to use."* When you celebrate a different benefit each time it keeps the Choice Process fresh.

This phrase completes the Choice Process. The purpose of saying these phrases is to change the way we think, which will lead to changed behavior. Remind yourself that abstinence brings reward and using again brings punishment (loss of benefits); this is crucial to renewing your mind.

Figure it out

So I can get my _____

(This phrase helps you with motivation)

What does it mean to embrace "The New Me?"

How can you make the Choice Process "fresh" each time you repeat it?

If you are a person of faith how can you bring God into your recovery?

It's time to grab your token and recite your Choice Process. Read it out loud several times:

"I want to use, I can use, however once and it's over. So in this moment I choose to accept temporary discomfort so I can get my benefits."

Chapter 11

Underlying Causes

There are reasons why we do what we do

"Addiction is the search for emotional satisfaction -- for a sense of security, a sense of being loved, even a sense of control over life. But the gratification is temporary and illusory, and the behavior results instead in greater self-disgust, reduced psychological security, and poorer coping ability. That's what all addictions have in common." **Stanton Peele, September 01, 2010, Psychology Today magazine**

There are always reasons why we do what we do. When an addict is asked, *"Why do you use?"* They will usually say, *"Because it feels good,"* which is true. A rush of dopamine to the brain always brings pleasure. However, there is much more to addiction than just enjoying a chemical reaction in the cerebral hemisphere.

Addiction is always about control. The sensation that substance abuse produces can become a very efficient way to regulate feelings, cope with stress, and experience emotion. Conventional wisdom says that people abuse alcohol or drugs in order to "numb out" and not feel. This can be true, however, most of the time people use so they CAN feel; for example: The alcoholic who can only cry when she has had too much to drink; the pot smoker who must take a few bong hits in order to be in touch with his creative side; the opiate user who can express his innermost emotions only when he is under the influence; and the cocaine addict who lets her hair down, gets loose on the dance floor, and becomes the life of the party only when she is high. What all of these people have in common is the tendency to rely on their addiction in order to emote.

There is always some type of underlying cause for substance abuse and addictive behavior. Each addict must introspectively start digging underneath to discover theirs, or they are in danger of experiencing relapse. Chemical dependency is very reliable; it's like a light switch on the wall that can be turned on with a flick of a finger. Take a hit, pop a pill, drink a shot, shoot up, or snort a line - then what happens? You feel good, each and every time. It can become so predictable and easy that you find you don't have to work at resolving conflict – just get high. You don't have to manage stress in a healthy way – just cop a buzz. You don't have to find something wholesome to do when you are bored – just get drunk. What about fun and happy times? Well, the addict learns that regular activities like camping trips, concerts and sporting events would be even MORE fun if you are using, so the natural joy of experiencing life always needs to be supplemented and enhanced.

Take a moment to consider the following emotional situations where addiction becomes an efficient way to cope:

> **The stress of responsibilities** – I use so I can control my stress levels that come from work pressures, frustrations, problems, obligations.

> **Loneliness, Depression** - I want to feel good physically and emotionally. So, I have turned to drugs as a substitute for a healthy life experience. Feeling high takes the edge off my loneliness; however, sometimes it makes me ache even more.

> **Anxiety** - Everyday life becomes a struggle and simple things become too much to handle. I have turned to drugs to help me deal with it. My drug of choice facilitates that escape. I am too wound up inside, both physically and mentally, so I act out to help me relax, calm down, or help me sleep.

> **Need for acceptance** - I feel rejected by significant others in my life, however, I have found a group of "friends" (fellow addicts) who accept me, like me, or desire me. But in reality, they don't care that I am killing myself.

> **I deserve a reward** – I don't have other pleasurable or fun outlets, so I rely on the feelings I get from my addiction to reward myself, help me enjoy life, and put me in a good mood.

> **To escape feelings of hurt** – I act out because it substitutes pleasure for the pain I am experiencing, particularly the pain of loneliness, loss, or hopelessness

➢ **To get attention** – I want others to notice me and so I misbehave to gain attention. I want others to see me as being wild and uninhibited – not pent up.

➢ **To punish myself** – I become enslaved to addiction because I believe I am really bad, sick, guilty, or not worthy. As my addictive behavior takes its toll, I don't care because I really believe that I deserve the self-punishment I am subjecting myself to.

➢ **To express my anger** – I use because I am retaliating against the expectations that others have of me, and because I know it will upset them. I want to get back at them for the pain they have caused me.

➢ **To be in control** – When I act out and use, I feel that I am in charge. Nobody can tell me not to. If I feel repressed by others who may not approve, I can then rebel against their attempts to control me by exercising something that they can't control - my addictive behavior.

The need for control is a big one for many people. As I explored my own underlying causes, I was surprised to find how big this one was for me personally. For me, addiction was not so much about substance; it was about my need to feel like I was in control. Growing up, I felt stifled by rules and regulations. I felt I was living in an overly regimented atmosphere, where everyone was telling me what I couldn't do, instead of empowering me to make choices about what I could do. It really doesn't matter if my upbringing was too strict or not, what mattered was my perception of my reality. I felt powerless and hemmed in. So, what was my reaction? I came to the conclusion that I would act out in order to take control. I didn't really understand what I was doing at the time, however; in my young, foolish, adolescent mind I thought I was justified. My thought process went something like this: *"I'm going to exhibit my own power and I'm going to do something these authority figures have no control over. I'm going to be as bad as I want to be. I'm going to do something that violates THEIR values."* So I went out, found someone who would provide marijuana and alcohol, and my pathway to addiction began.

Addiction and deceit often go hand in hand. The addict must become very proficient at lying and covering his tracks in order to continue to use. This also can be very exciting, a high all its own. You can become addicted to the thrill of "putting one over" on others, especially if you are in a situation where you have to hide your addiction from a parent, employer, loved ones, or spouse. Keeping your addiction going can become a game of chess, where you are in a constant strategic mode, and thinking three moves ahead of other people who might find out what you are doing. If you become good at hiding, this brings on a feeling of control that can be exciting. It won't be long until the thrill of getting away with using becomes just as rewarding as using itself.

Sometimes you can involve yourself in addictive behavior to punish yourself. You may have come to believe that you are a bad person; unworthy of love, guilty, and not deserving of good things or happiness. As addictive behavior begins to takes its toll, you might not even care, because you have come to believe that you deserve the self-punishment that you are subjecting yourself to. Some people engage in a destructive behavior called "cutting": Injuring yourself on purpose by making scratches or cuts on your body with a sharp object. People who cut may not have developed normal and healthy ways to cope, or their coping skills may be overpowered by emotions that are too intense. When emotions don't get expressed in a healthy way, tension can build up — sometimes to a point where it seems almost unbearable. Cutting can become a coping mechanism to relieve that extreme tension. For some, it can seem to bring about a feeling of control. When an individual cuts on their self what is going on inside? Cutting creates an endorphin release in the brain, because injury makes your adrenaline flow. You can become addicted to that particular type of high that the cutting experience creates. However, as we begin to explore the various possibilities for underlying causes of someone who cuts, perhaps they are wanting to punish themselves for an unmet expectation – either their own or someone else's. Or, the underlying cause may be to express anger. They may think to themselves: *"I will cut because I know it would upset others, and perhaps they would pay attention to my pain. I want to get back at them for the anguish they've caused me."* In either case it's all about control.

In Chapter 7 we discussed how our addiction can become our "friend." We turn to our "friend" when we are happy, sad, stressed, lonely, bored, or angry. The feeling from engaging in addictive substances or behaviors becomes a "surrogate" emotional pacifier, instead of experiencing and expressing those feelings through relationships, which is God's naturally designed outlet. Emotional connection through relationship is the natural way to experience life's many ups and downs. However, substance abuse can become a way to efficiently control feelings so that relationships with others are put on hold. When addiction drags on for years, personal growth is also put on hold. Many people who have struggled with addiction since the teen years are stuck in "emotional adolescence" even as an adult. When you finally choose to stop you will need to play "catch up" in your emotional intelligence. This means that you will need to learn to turn to friends, family, or spouse to process your feelings, instead of the addiction. Doing so can be quite a challenge because, in some cases, perhaps you have never really experienced true emotional intimacy and wouldn't even know what it looks or feels like. Your addiction has proficiently, but destructively, filled that relational void for you.

Consequently, part of addressing addiction is looking at underlying causes. If you don't, you endanger yourself for relapse or for something that I call "substitution." Substitution is when you exchange one addiction for another. You stop crack cocaine but turn to meth. You stop abusing prescription drugs, but then your drinking escalates. Substitution can happen when underlying causes are not addressed.

For example: In my situation, I smoked pot for about 10 years when I was younger. There came a day when I quit. I stopped smoking marijuana "cold turkey." I celebrated victory over my addiction! Or so I thought.

Now, when I look back, I can see that was also the time when my drinking, which had been fairly casual, social and moderate, escalated and became a problem. I just substituted one addiction for another, because I never addressed the underlying causes to my addictive behavior. Years later, I stopped drinking, but then turned to a sugar addiction shortly afterwards. Some times when people stop drinking, because of hypoglycemia that is often a result of their alcohol consumption, they will become addicted to sweets. Food addiction (especially sugar) is another way to regulate your emotional state by relying on the "feel good" chemicals of the brain that come from eating a candy bar or consuming a hot fudge sundae.

The Bible declares, "... *a man out to examine himself...*"[10] Socrates once said, *"A life unexamined is not worth living."* This is why, in order for addiction recovery to be well balanced, there must also be soul searching. Self-examination remains the single most important aspect of lasting recovery. People go to therapy when they're stuck in a depression, mired by anxiety, or struggling in their marriage, but when someone is addicted often there is the narrow view that all that needs to take place is for the addictive behavior to stop. This is short-sighted and inaccurate. Through counseling and self-examination we're able to expand our awareness of our blind spots. These are the hidden parts that you are unaware of, but they create major problems that often manifest themselves through relationships. It's most common for an addict to become troubled about their addiction because of relational repercussions. By

---

[10] 1 Corinthians 11:28a, The New International Version of the Holy Bible

becoming aware of your past, and exploring your inner fears courageously, you can find the avenue to total renewal--this is where deep and lasting growth takes place. Those who engage in counseling consistently express one thing - *surprise* - over seeing themselves in a way they had not previously. A good counselor or therapist will help you see your motives, your struggles, your brokenness, and your beauty. Good counseling offers a mirror that reflects the depth of the soul. It's a way of standing in your own presence and becoming aware.

The purpose of this chapter is to shed light on the importance of self-examination so that you can discover your own underlying causes of addiction. This is best accomplished with a counselor familiar with addictions. If you are not in a program or currently working with a qualified counselor who can guide you through this introspective process, then I can't emphasis strongly enough how important this is for you to make happen. Today, get on the phone and find someone to help you discover any barriers you have to having the life you desire. Take this book with you and work through it with your counselor. Self-examination is power to make permanent changes.

"Wisdom is supreme; therefore get wisdom. Though it cost all you have, get understanding."[11] There are always reasons we do what we do. Those reasons are called "underlying causes." What are yours?

Figure it out

- Addiction is always about _____.

How would you define the term: "underlying cause" when it comes to addiction?

_____

_____

_____

Why is it important for someone to know and become aware of their underlying causes?

_____

_____

_____

---

[11] Proverbs 4:7 The New International Version of the Holy Bible

How has your addiction enabled you to cope emotionally and relationally?

_____

_____

_____

Can you identify at least one of your own underlying causes? Describe it here:

_____

_____

_____

What is "substitution" and how might that happen to you?

_____

_____

_____

It's time to grab your token and recite your Choice Process. Read it out loud several times:

"I want to use, I can use, however once and it's over. So in this moment I choose to accept temporary discomfort so I can get my benefits.

Chapter 12

Face it!

DISCLAIMER: *The content discussed in this chapter should only be considered when you have fully engaged in all aspects of the Choice Process presented thus far, and ideally, with the guidance of a qualified counselor. In addition, you should have made a decision, based on your thorough understanding of the Choice Process and whole-hearted participation in the ideas and philosophies presented in this book that says you are ready to face your addiction with confidence. Facing your addiction prematurely, and without proper planning, could be counter-productive and lead to relapse. Please use discretion.*

You will never gain control over anything that you run from. When beginning recovery in the early days of sobriety, avoiding situations where you might 'use' is important, because you have not yet learned how to control your urge. But this is not a good, long term plan. We avoid people, places or things because we say, *"If I hang out over there then I might get an urge to use and then I am going to relapse, so I better stay home."* The reality is, that sooner or later, you are going to experience an urge to use whether you stay at home, take a walk in the park, go to work, or out to a party. And when urge meets opportunity, if you are not prepared properly, you face a high probability for relapse. So, what is the solution? Learn to deal with the urge by facing it and not avoiding it.

So let's review: In chapter six we learned about The Cycle of Deprivation, where stopping is the punishment and using again becomes the reward. The Cycle of Deprivation has a lot to do with your urge to use. The urge starts to build, and it grows stronger and stronger. The urge is uncomfortable, it's hard, and it seems almost unbearable; so we hate the urge, and we loathe it. We wish it would dry up and go away, and we pray for it to disappear, but it continues to build. Perhaps an individual can exercise will-power and stave off the urge for a while, but pretty soon he will cave in and use, thus completing the cycle where stopping was the punishment and using again becomes the reward.

Most traditional treatment programs will tell you: *"Okay, you've come here for help with addiction, we know what the problem is: The problem is your urge. So, here is what we want you to do about that urge: We want you to avoid* <u>*people*</u>, <u>*places,*</u> *or* <u>*things*</u> *that you associate with using, because you might find yourself in those situations and 'trigger', and then ultimately relapse."* This type of conventional wisdom is explained as follows: You need to avoid people in your life that might influence you to use. Next, you need to avoid places where you have used in the past. So, if your problem is alcohol, avoid restaurants that serve alcoholic beverages. Plan to take different routes to and from work to keep yourself away from places where you used to drink. And finally, avoid any things that you might do associated with your addiction. For example, if you like to bowl, but each time you bowl you always drink, then it would be best to give up bowling because of that association. In all fairness, since this type of philosophy is based on the idea that one is powerless and diseased for life, then avoiding and sequestering would be the only viable solution. In other words the problem is that pesky urge, so do whatever you can to avoid it. Don't think about it; don't do anything that might "trigger it." Learn to fear it and repress it, and if you do that long enough you will be okay. However, the problem is not outside of you, the problem is inside of you.

So far in this book, many of the things you have read might have struck you as counter-intuitive to what you have believed or what you have learned previously. Statements like: "I want to use" or "I can use" are not normally used in conventional treatment program methodology. It is my belief that our culture gives addiction too much power. When we counsel people to live in fear of their addiction, we are just exchanging one enslavement for another. I don't think that is a good plan for personal freedom.

Treatment philosophies that are based on avoidance and repression keep people enslaved to a lifestyle of fear. Avoidance is a way of sequestering yourself from the opportunity to use. Repression is intentionally distracting oneself from the urge when it comes to mind. Avoidance and repression can be helpful in the beginning of your journey toward freedom, but they will not serve you well in the long run. What does avoidance and repression look like? For example: Let's say you have a shopping addiction. Conventional wisdom dictates that, whatever you do don't go to the mall, especially with your credit card. If you have a drinking problem, don't be around others who drink, and avoid all restaurants that serve alcohol. Do you have an online problem? Let someone else place a password on your computer to control your behavior instead of exercising your power of choice. What if you have a gambling problem? Certainly you would break out in a cold sweat at the thought of a layover in Las Vegas, so you better book another flight that has a layover in an alternate city. So, in this line of reasoning, you would avoid all situations where you might experience an urge, and when experiencing an urge you should never allow yourself to think about it; instead, distract yourself by working out, watching a movie or calling your sponsor.

But wait a minute! Isn't it wise to run from trouble? Yes, there is a time to run and there also is a time to stand and fight. I am suggesting that you consider fighting for your sobriety by "facing the giant" of your addiction head on, in a controlled, systematic way, that will allow you to live in complete freedom for a lifetime.

Every person who has experienced the pain and consequences of addiction, and then is able to enjoy a period of sobriety, battles with fear of relapse along the path of their journey. The fear of relapsing sounds like this:

"I am enjoying not drinking today but the annual Christmas party is coming up; what if I am weak and take a drink while I am there?"

" I have finally kicked the habit and I am loving how I feel, but what if I find myself in a situation where I get an offer to get high again? Will I be strong enough to say no?"

"*I am doing great now but my spouse and the kids will be going to grandma's house for a few days leaving me all alone - what if I use?*"

"*I have a business trip coming up next month; that was always a time when I would binge. This is part of my job and I have to go, but I am scared to death.*"

"*Things are terrific right now so it feels easy to stay sober. However, what if I have a hard day at work? What if I get in an argument with my spouse? What if I face major stress? I fear I will go back to my old ways.*"

"*In the past I would tell my spouse that I was going to the store, and then while I was out I would use. I am afraid I might pick up right where I left off before recovery. Maybe I shouldn't go to the store or do errands alone anymore.*"

Notice the similarities with each of these concerns: Fear of the urge and fear of the future. Walking in fear is not God's design for humanity. There is a wise saying in the Bible: "*For you did not receive a spirit that makes you a slave again to fear...*"[12] The title of this book is "Figure it, Face it and Fix it." There IS a cure for addiction – you CAN "fix it." The first chapters of this book escorted you along a journey towards "figuring" out the problem and answering the questions of why you do what you do. Now,

---

[12] Romans 8:15a The New International Version of the Holy Bible

in order for this problem to be fixed, you must face your addiction. You cannot fix a problem by running from it. Facing your fears is the final step to unlocking the chains of addiction that will lead you to the life of freedom you desire.

When used in the context of clinical psychology, the word for fear is "phobia." One of the most common and successful techniques in behavior therapy today to treat anxiety disorders and phobia is called Exposure Therapy. The technique of this type of therapy is to slowly over time, expose a patient to what they fear, until they have rewired the brain to not be fearful anymore. The goal in exposure therapy is to create anxiety, but only a small amount; too much and they will run away or shut down. Exposure Therapy allows you to face your fear for just the right amount of time and intensity so your brain learns that even though you experienced the emotion of fear you will not die or be harmed. When you are exposed to your fear in a controlled way, then your brain updates its belief system.

For example: Let's say that when you were very young, you were mauled by a neighborhood dog that had gotten loose and it was very traumatic for you. Ever since then, you have been afraid of dogs. In fact, your fear was so intense that you would take the trouble to cross the

street to avoid a neighbor who might be walking his dog –
even if it was on a leash. But now you are married with
young children and your spouse and kids have been
talking about getting a family pet, a dog. You don't want to
deny your family the fun of owning and caring for an
animal, so you come to me for Exposure Therapy to
overcome your fear. Now, I happen to own a large dog and
he is penned up on my property next to my counseling
office. So, when you arrive for your first appointment I
have you visualize being around a dog. Just thinking
about it in your mind creates anxiety – this is good. On
your next appointment, we will take our chairs outside so
you can sit and see the dog in the pen. This might create
more anxiety in you, but as you sit there you realize the
dog is locked up and you will not be harmed, so you feel
calm by the end of our session. The next time you come,
we take our chairs and have our session right in front of
the gate of the pen. This creates much agitation for you,
but you hang in there and by the end of the hour it barely
bothers you to sit so close. At subsequent sessions we
actually go in the pen and our graduation session is a
successful trip to the dog park, where you pet all types of
dogs with no fear at all.   This is an example of how
Exposure Therapy works. Notice that on the first visit I
did not take you near the dog right away. We started in the

mind, and then added other senses in a slow, systematic fashion that culminated in a full sensory experience of seeing, hearing, smelling, and touching canines.

When it comes to overcoming your fear of relapse, we can do the same exercise. The first step always begins in the mind. I want you to go through your "using ritual" from start to finish in your psyche. Every addict has a ritual. A ritual is how you go about using. Rituals often start out first thing in the morning and then culminate with the first hit, drink, fix, snort, huff, or swallow. For example: My ritual, when I was drinking, started first thing in the morning when I got up. I was already planning how I was going to get my drink of choice by deciding when and how I would stop off at the little convenience store to buy the bottle. Then I needed to plan my day, to make sure I could start drinking at 5pm. (I never drank before 5 because that is what alcoholics did and I was sure I was not an alcoholic....DENIAL!!!) At 5pm, I made sure I was in a place where I would not be seen, and I cracked open the bottle, smelled that familiar scent of tequila, and then took that first drink. As I felt the burn of the alcohol on the back of my throat and began to feel the early experience of the familiar buzz, I would look at the bottle in my hands: The familiar gold and yellow label, the amber liquid, and the trails of the alcohol dripping down the inside of the glass bottle. Every aspect of this experience added up to be part of my ritual: Planning, purchasing, preparing, and pouring. I was fully engaged emotionally, physically, and mentally. Emotionally, I felt the feelings of: Anxiety to use, anticipation to drink, and excitement to catch a buzz. As I neared the 5:00 hour, my body began to react physically: A rise in my blood pressure, dry mouth, sweaty palms, and physical agitation as I knew my first drink was closer. The mental aspects of the ritual began in the morning as I strategized, planned, and deliberated over all the details of making sure I could get high.

Face it

Now it's your turn. What are the details of your ritual? Take a moment to go through the following exercise: Write down your thoughts about how you use. What is your strategy to 'score?' How do you prepare? Describe the details of what you do when you get high: Where are you? What are you doing? What are your surroundings like? Who are you with? What are the sights, sounds, smells and feelings? Be as thorough and complete as possible.

_____

_____

_____

_____

_____

_____

_____

_____

_____

_____

_____

_____

Now let's examine the urge itself - Write down how you feel when the urge to use is at its strongest. What is going on for you emotionally, physically and mentally?

EMOTIONALLY	PHYSICALLY	MENTALLY
1.	1.	1.
2.	2.	2.
3.	3.	3.
4.	4.	4.

Now it's time to recite the Choice Process. Hopefully you have it memorized by now:

"I want to use, I can use, however once and it's over. So in this moment I choose to accept temporary discomfort so I can get my benefits."

Congratulations, you have just done the first level of "work" that will set you free from the fear of relapse and the enslavement of your addiction. Instead of running from the urge, we created the urge. We brought it up from the subconscious mind to the forefront of your thinking. Although it was just in your mind, this was a powerful exercise that allowed you to face your addiction. Take special note how you ended the exercise: With reciting the Choice Process. Repeating your Choice Process after facing an urge, is an important part of doing "work." We are reinforcing new ways of thinking.

Re-creating your ritual in the mind would be an example of "low level work." Everyone should be able to engage in this type of work. The next step is to consider if you are ready for a medium level of work. Medium level work puts you in the proximity of facing your addiction in a carefully thought out and controlled fashion. Examples of medium level work might be:

An alcoholic that goes to the grocery market: Instead of avoiding the liquor aisle, he chooses to walk down it, perhaps even picking up his drink of choice and holding it. One might even take the bottle, put it in his cart, and wheel around shopping for other items on the list. When he is done with the exercise he can return the bottle.

The addict who drives by the home of their dealer, perhaps even parks outside. You know he is in the house; he is home and he has your drug of choice. All you need to do is walk up to the door and knock...

Choose to attend your local Alcoholics Anonymous meeting. Many people report a rise in their urge to use when listening to the various testimonies of those who share their story of drug and alcohol abuse.

In each one of these situations, it is important to do the work and then while you are engaging your urge, recite the Choice Process phrases. Reciting your Choice Process affirms your commitment to the truth of what is happening within you, and the reality of why you are choosing to abstain. Doing work without including your Choice Process phraseology would be incomplete; don't leave out the most important part of doing the work.

"But..." someone might protest. *"...what if the alcoholic takes that bottle to the cashier and buys it? What if the addict walks up to the dealer's door, knocks and enters the house?"* If they do, they will lose their benefits. Remember the phrase: "However, once and it's over?" It's not like that opportunity won't be there sometime in the near future. All we are doing with this exercise is creating the opportunity, in a controlled situation, before it actually happens. We are doing "work." When you face your addiction, you are empowered to not fear relapse; this is freedom, and this is our goal.

Whenever I talk with a client about engaging in "work," I make it very clear that any work they do must be their idea – not mine. I make suggestions, guide the process, and brain-storm ideas, but I do not pressure a person or decide what their work will look like for them, or even if they will participate in the exercise. An individual MUST be ready to do this for himself. Before suggesting a client engages in doing medium or high level work, I make sure we have gone through the Choice Process teaching and the individual is at a place where they are ready. Timing is everything, and jumping into "work" too soon may prove counter-productive.

The final stage of Exposure Therapy would be defined as "high level work." Not all clients participate at this level – nor should they. Again, each individual must decide for themselves whether or not this kind of exposure would be valuable for them or wise to do. I would estimate that about 30 to 40% of my clients choose to participate at this level, and those who do, often express a profound sense of accomplishment and a wonderful feeling of freedom from the fear of relapse. High level work involves placing yourself in a situation where you come face to face with your addiction, in a carefully thought out method. When you enter into this level of work, you must come at it from a position of strength, not weakness. Those who engage in high level work completely understand and have gotten control over their "Junkie Mind;" they have memorized their Choice Process and have thoroughly enjoyed the benefits of their sobriety for a reasonable period of time. They are ready to stare down the barrel of the "gun" that used to threaten their very existence. Allow me to give you some examples of medium or high level work: (names have been changed to protect privacy)

Mary – Mary was a binge drinker. Her job required lots of travel to convention centers in many U.S. cities. She averaged a business trip about every four to six weeks. Between travel times, Mary was the consummate housewife, spouse and parent. She rarely drank while at home; however, business travel was a different story. Mary's ritual was to "Google" her next business destination and find the nearest liquor store located near her hotel. Upon arrival, she would rent a car and travel directly to the liquor store, buy a bottle of vodka, and then check into her room. Being a "functional alcoholic," she would do her business successfully during the day, but drink heavily late into the night. At the appropriate time in her treatment, Mary decided to plan an upcoming business trip to Miami Beach to do high level work. She followed her ritual to the letter and soon found herself in her hotel room with a large bottle of vodka sitting on the end table. Mary was scheduled to be there for three days. For the first two nights, she poured herself a glass of vodka "straight up" in the hotel room glass they provide for water. (This was part of her ritual.) She sat and watched TV with the full glass of vodka only an arm's length away. The smell wafted over to her nose. The sight of the clear liquid and the understanding that she was all alone – no accountability – was all an important part of her "work." Several times during the evening, she would pick up the glass, recite her Choice Process, and then return the glass to the table. Each night, she then poured it down the sink before retiring to bed at a decent hour. Late on the third night she took the remaining bottle of vodka out on the deserted beach next to her hotel and ritually poured it out on the sand. She later told me, *"That was the most empowering thing I have ever done in my life. If I can do this I can do anything."*

Joe – Joe loved to play pool with his friends down at the local bar. He had a tight group of friends who would meet each weekend for some friendly games. Of course, part of the experience was drinking beer as they shot pool together. At the appropriate time in Joe's recovery we began to discuss whether or not he might like to participate in one of the various levels of work. Since alcohol was Joe's challenge he was worried that he would have to stop going to the bar and playing pool with his friends, now that he had made the choice to remain sober. The conversation went something like this:

Joe – *"Well, I guess I won't be able to play pool with my friends any longer."*

Me – *"Why not?"*

Joe – *"Because, I can't go into a bar, now that I have stopped drinking."*

Me – *"Just because you go into a bar does not automatically mean you are going to drink – right?"*

Joe – *"Hmmm, I suppose so. I can always order a soft drink or water."*

Me – *"You could, or you could take this opportunity to do some 'work.' What if you settled into a night of pool playing with your friends and ordered a beer."*

Joe – *"But what if I drank it?"*

Me – *"What if you did? You want to and you can, but I would like to think that in that moment you will choose temporary discomfort so you can get your benefits and just leave it on the table while you play your game."*

Joe – *"I suppose I could see myself do that. But what happens when the waitress comes around and asks if I am ready for another?"*

Me – *"You don't need to explain anything. Just tell her, 'Thanks, I'm good right now."*

Joe – *"But what if my friends notice I am not drinking the beer."*

Me – *"If they happen to notice, then just tell them you're doing fine, thanks for asking, but you're good. If they really are your friends they will leave you alone."*

So, Joe thought it through, planned his work, and enjoyed a night out with his friends playing pool. To his surprise, his friends didn't even notice that his beer went untouched and the waitress stopped asking after the first inquiry. All throughout the evening, he would glance over at the table, notice the frosty beer with the condensation dripping down the side and then recite his Choice Process quietly to himself. Joe told me that as he left the bar, he remembered looking back at the full beer left on the table and decided that instead of regarding the exercise as a waste of money (because the beer went untouched) he decided that the money spent was the best investment of his life. He was empowered by the experience and felt he went *"five levels deeper in his commitment to enjoying a sober life."*

Fred - It all started with a simple, outpatient surgery and a prescription of Oxycodone to manage the pain for a few days. Taking pills orally then led to crushing and smoking the powder sprinkled on a joint. From there, Fred discovered the most powerful and quickest method to get high was to inject himself with a needle. Recovery for Fred was a long journey. I first started working with him when he was in the throes of detox. Fred took to the program and participated well in learning the Choice Process, exploring his underlying causes and engaging in low to medium levels of work. During treatment, Fred explained his ritual in great detail. He talked about scoring the drug, then where he would park his car and begin preparing his fix. The climax of his routine came when he would stick the needle in his arm, pull back on the plunger and see a small cloud of blood in the barrel of the syringe. This meant that he had hit a vein and it would only be seconds before he would depress the plunger, injecting the drug into his blood stream, where he would feel its powerful effects. At the appropriate time in his program, when Fred felt he was ready, we began to discuss the possibility of engaging in high level work. At first, Fred wanted to score some "Oxys" and go through all the stages of his ritual short of shooting up. However, when dealing with illegal drug use, I never want to encourage illegal behavior. There are ways to engage in various levels of work without violating the law or jeopardizing your freedom. So, after much deliberation, Fred decided on an alternate plan. It was important to Fred to take himself all the way to the climax of his ritual, in order to face his addiction. So, after careful planning Fred chose the day and time where he would do his own work. Fred loaded the syringe with saline solution, then pulled back the plunger and saw the familiar cloud of blood in the barrel. He recited the Choice Process, withdrew the needle and squeezed out the liquid onto the ground. I asked Fred how he felt about his experience. He told me that right afterwards it didn't seem like that big of a deal, but as he thought about what he had accomplished, it became more and more profound.

When engaging in high level work for someone who is breaking their addiction to illegal drugs, I recommend using a "placebo substance" for the exercise. There is great benefit in engaging all the senses in the work process: What you do with your hands, what your eyes see and what your ears hear. Pot smokers can take oregano and roll a joint. Cocaine users can substitute baking soda and go through the whole process of cutting and lining on a glass coffee table or mirror. Those who shoot up can fill their "rig" with saline solution. The important aspects of high level work is to create a strong urge, face it, recite your Choice Process, and finish with a celebration of victory.

The question is often asked, *"How many times do you have to engage in work?"* You will know. For some, it's just one time. Others may choose several different encounters. The bottom line is that you will know when work is no longer needed. You will know when you are done.

There are those who may find this concept difficult to understand. They may even think that it's reckless or crazy. But it is neither. Done at the right time, and under the proper circumstances, this aspect of The Choice Process is the brilliance of what makes the program so powerful. Please note that this type of Exposure Therapy is not mentioned in the first few chapters, but is revealed near the end. In order to ensure success, make sure you are working from a position of strength, not weakness and you will find this might be the exercise that unlocks the life of freedom you have desired.

Face it

Describe what **low level work** might look like to you?

How about **medium level work**? What would that look like?

As you read this chapter and contemplate the idea of "work" (especially the higher levels of "work") how does it make you feel? Circle the words below that best represent your emotional reaction:

Afraid   Capable   Nervous   Spirited
        Fragile   Positive   Bewildered
Brave   Turned off   Eager   Powerless
        Worried   Determined

Now, take a look at the words that you have circled on the previous page. If you picked emotions that are hopeful and optimistic, then you might be ready for the higher levels of work. If you picked emotions that are hesitant and cautious, then you probably should stick with the lower levels for now.

High level work (describe what you envision as detailed as you can)

Remember, work would not be complete or productive without reciting your Choice Process.

"I want to use, I can use, however once and it's over. So in this moment I choose to accept temporary discomfort so I can get my benefits."

Chapter 13
Fix it
Preventing relapse
And getting the life you want

When something is broken we explore how it can be fixed. If addiction is a disease, then shouldn't we be looking for a cure? The idea of defining addiction as a disease has been debated for several years. For some it can be controversial, because we usually think of a disease as something you "catch;" and therefore it is out of your control and you are devoid of personal responsibility because you are "sick." However, our society has no problem classifying heart disease or diabetes as diseases, and yet we see them largely acquired through life style related health choices. A person may have a genetic pre-disposition to heart disease or diabetes, but that doesn't mean they are going to get those diseases automatically. However, if one makes enough high risk choices concerning diet and exercise then you put yourself at much greater risk.

Addiction is often seen as a "brain disease." If you make enough high risk choices, you can alter your brain chemistry and neuro-chemical system, creating an actual physiological problem that needs to be addressed. So, in other words, chronic addiction can lead to brain disease. This doesn't mean you are off the hook for personal responsibility. No, the addict bears responsibility of creating this problem, because they have made high risk choices that have led to neurological impairment. However, we know that with many diseases there is a cure and addiction is no exception.

Because the problem of addiction lies primarily in the brain, a well balanced approach to recovery should address overall brain health, brain nutrition and neurological chemical balance. Medical science has found that many prescription drugs can aid the treatment process when it comes to withdrawal, recovery, and relapse prevention. For heavy opiate users, chronic meth use, and long term cocaine abuse, many people experience depression, the blues, or a "blah" feeling once they become clean and sober. This is primarily because the addict has been over-taxing their dopamine receptors and they are not designed for that kind of continual abuse. This feeling is only temporary while the brain heals. However, it may take as much as a year for that healing to take place. In the meantime, you might consider working with your family practitioner or a psychiatrist who can prescribe medication to help you through the harder times. Just knowing that these symptoms may occur and understanding that they are only temporary may help an individual to hang in there, while they rebuild their life and heal their body.

I also recommend placing yourself in the care of a good naturopathic doctor, who can help you design a healthy homeopathic regimen for healing the damage that has been caused by chronic chemical or alcohol abuse. Certain vitamins and supplements can improve your overall health, diminish cravings, and help in relapse prevention using natural herbs and nutrients. A proper diet and a healthy exercise regimen will prove invaluable to getting yourself back to optimum health. A healthy body translates into confidence, which leads to a stronger mindset about staying the course and preventing relapse.

Imagine you are hiking along a sharp ridgeline and there is a deep valley on either side. If you get off the pathway in either direction, you place yourself in danger of falling over the steep embankment into the gorge below. Let's call the valley on your left side, "walking in fear," and the valley on the right side we will label, "false confidence." Staying on the pathway is called "walking in freedom." In Chapter 12, we discussed why Exposure Therapy can help an individual to overcome fear, so they don't have to move forward in life afraid that they might "trigger" and lose all their benefits at any moment. My hope for you is that you will not walk in fear; walking in fear diminishes your overall quality of life. The exercises in the previous chapter are designed to help you avoid that pitfall, and stay on the freedom path.

False confidence is an attitude that says, *"I've got this whipped."* Someone who slips into the valley of false confidence has lost the meaning and power behind the truth statement, "once and it's over." From time to time, you will hear stories of people who have been clean and sober for years and then go back to using. They fell into the valley of false confidence, believing the lie of the Junkie Mind that they could go back to using and it will be okay. Beware of false confidence; it will be waiting for you around the corner – maybe after several years of sobriety.

There is a difference between walking in fear and living in false confidence, and that's the middle pathway of freedom. The freedom path is an attitude of self-assurance that is neither fearful nor cocky. It's wonderful to feel positive and confident about your progress, but sometimes that can be carried too far. If someone stops using their Choice Process because they think they are "all done," this could be a sign of false confidence. It's like a musician who plays guitar and says, *"I already know how to play; I don't need to practice anymore."* Sooner or later they will lose their edge. You need to deal with your addiction on an ongoing basis at some level, by regularly reciting the "Choice Process" and celebrating the benefits you have grown to love.

If you have engaged yourself in the principles of this book, you no doubt have seen personal growth happen. Perhaps this is the first time in a long time that you have enjoyed the benefits of making changes. In order to get the life you want, you will need to continue your personal growth. In order to achieve that, dedicate yourself to being a life-long learner. Always have a plan for growth. That plan might include reading books, enjoying seminars, taking a class, or finding someone to mentor you. Getting the life you want requires a dedication to movement. Don't allow yourself to stagnate. Adopt the value of bringing your best self to your marriage, your parenting, your friendships, your career, and your Creator.

I firmly believe that God has a plan and a purpose for every human being. Do you know what your purpose is? Why are you here on this earth? Here is a principle that I live by: "from your pain comes your purpose." Addiction has brought me lots of pain over the years; however, it was from that pain that I experienced wisdom and insight so I could "pay it forward," helping others who are struggling. If you are going through a painful divorce, who might minister to you the most? The person who has been through their own divorce and is now on the upside of that experience. If you are a cancer patient who is undergoing chemotherapy, who might empathize best with your pain? A cancer survivor, of course!

It's been said, *"God never wastes a hurt."* As you walk in freedom from your addiction, my encouragement to you is to come alongside someone else who is struggling like you were, and guide them through the principles you have learned in this book. The Choice Process is a life skill. Use the truth principles found in these simple phrases to help yourself, and others, achieve the life you were designed to fulfill. May God bless your journey.

Fix it

What do you think about addiction as a "disease?" What are the pros and cons for this kind of labeling?

Define in your own words the principle of "false confidence."

What is your plan to become a "lifelong learner?" List three goals below that you would like to accomplish in the next 6 months.

1. _____

2. _____

3. _____

What is your life purpose? Why are you on the earth?
What have you been designed by God to do, to help
others? Use the space below to write out your thoughts.

By now you should know your Choice Process without
even looking.

*"I want to use, I can use, however once and it's over.
So in this moment I choose to accept temporary
discomfort so I can get my benefits."*

Answers to study questions

Chapter 2 –
- Answers: motivated, admit, yourself, selfish

Chapter 3 –
- Answers: systematic, think, actions, information, conviction

Chapter 4 –
- Answers: truth, declarative, your addiction, memorize

Chapter 5 –
- Answers: <u>WANT</u>, truth, personal, obsessing, denial, help

Chapter 6 –
- Answers: <u>CAN</u>, Choice, deprivation
- some common feelings may be: anger, jealousy, shame, frustration, missing out, etc.

Chapter 7 –
- What is over? Your benefits

Chapter 8
So in this <u>MOMENT</u>

What is the "Junkie Mind? - That part of you who will do anything to get you to use again. We "personify" The Junkie Mind so you can visualize the dialogue that happens inside your mind. The Junkie Mind is smart, cunning and always works in the future.

Why is "getting out in the future", when it comes to stopping, a pitfall? - The Junkie Mind wants you to get out into the future to panic you into using again. Obsession and fear about future use can create a feeling of futility where you might conclude, "What's the use, I might as well use."

Chapter 9 –
- Answers: top blanks: <u>ACCEPT</u>, <u>DISCOMFORT</u>

Why is the addiction urge perceived as a negative? - It makes you feel uncomfortable; you see no value in the urge. The key to gaining control is learning to accept the urge and making a choice about it.

How can you learn to "accept" the urge? - By retraining your mind to accept the discomfort as a positive sign that you are getting your benefits and a chance to "work" so you can gain control.

How one can view discomfort in a positive way? - Knowing the discomfort is only temporary

Chapter 10 -
- Answers: <u>BENEFITS</u>

What does it mean to embrace "The New Me?" - When we rewire our brain to embrace the benefits of abstinence as part of the "new me," the reward switches from using to not using. Therefore the choice to be abstinent comes from within and has long lasting results.

How can you make the Choice Process "fresh" each time you repeat it? - Each time you repeat The Choice Process pick a benefit and meditate on it.

If you are a person of faith how can you bring God into your recovery? - Pray back the Choice Process in the form of a prayer to God.

Chapter 11 –
- Answers: Addiction is always about <u>CONTROL.</u>

How would you define the term: "underlying cause" when it comes to addiction? - Underlying causes are the coping mechanism addiction provides that short circuit normal, healthy interactions with life.

Why is it important for someone to know and become aware of their underlying causes? - Without an understanding of your underlying causes you become at risk for relapse or substitution.

How has your addiction enabled you to cope emotionally and relationally? - In order to answer this question properly you must become introspective and take the time to examine yourself properly. This can happen efficiently with a good therapist or counselor.

Can you identify at least one of your own underlying causes? Describe it here: (If you cannot, you may not have done the work necessary to ensure sobriety for years to come.)

Definition of substitution: Stopping one addictive behavior and going on to another. This usually happens when the underlying causes for engaging in the addictive behavior go unaddressed.

Chapters 12 and 13 –
There is no "right" or "wrong" answers in these sections. I encourage you to take the time to think through each response using your own words. Don't rush the process, each question is carefully crafted to help you figure, face and fix your particular challenge.

Meet the author

Mark Turansky lives on the beautiful island of Oahu, Hawaii with his bride Cheryl and two daughters, Taylor and Rylie. A local resident since 1978, he loves Hawaii's beaches, motorsports racing and outdoor recreation.

Mark is Executive Director and owner of New Horizons Counseling in Hawaii with over 20 years of professional counseling experience. He is certified as an Addictions & Recovery Specialist, Wellness Counselor and Marriage Life Coach. Being trained as clergy, Mark got his start with counseling in the ministry, but soon began to see that he had a natural gifting for helping others.

Booking the author for
speaking engagements:

To contact the author:

www.figureitfaceitfixit.com

www.newhorizonshawaii.com

email: info@newhorizonshawaii.com

(808)484-1000

About New Horizons Counseling: (est. 1980) is a nationally recognized program that utilizes a cognitive approach for teaching individuals to make constructive, rather than destructive choices for drinking, drugs, or substance abuse. New Horizons is listed on the official SAMHSA (US Dept. Of Health and Human Services Substance abuse and mental health Services administration.)

New Horizons donation information
(FEIN #99-0354544) New Horizons Counseling came under the umbrella of the educational nonprofit - One Achord in 2009. One Achord is, 501(3C) organization established in 2001.

Did you enjoy this book?
Has it been helpful in your journey?
Please consider writing a review on
Amazon.com so others can benefit as well

Made in the USA
San Bernardino, CA
26 January 2014